An Atheist Reads the Torah: Secular Humanistic Perspectives on the Five Books of Moses

Alan M. Perlman, PhD

Order this book online at www.trafford.com/06-0056
or email orders@trafford.com

Most Trafford titles are also available at major online book retailers.

Note for Librarians: A cataloguing record for this book is available from Library and Archives Canada at www.collectionscanada.ca/amicus/index-e.html

ISBN: 978-1-4120-8301-0

We at Trafford believe that it is the responsibility of us all, as both individuals and corporations, to make choices that are environmentally and socially sound. You, in turn, are supporting this responsible conduct each time you purchase a Trafford book, or make use of our publishing services. To find out how you are helping, please visit www.trafford.com/responsiblepublishing.html

Our mission is to efficiently provide the world's finest, most comprehensive book publishing service, enabling every author to experience success. To find out how to publish your book, your way, and have it available worldwide, visit us online at www.trafford.com/10510

www.trafford.com

North America & international
toll-free: 1 888 232 4444 (USA & Canada)
phone: 250 383 6864 • fax: 250 383 6804 • email: info@trafford.com

The United Kingdom & Europe
phone: +44 (0)1865 722 113 • local rate: 0845 230 9601
facsimile: +44 (0)1865 722 868 • email: info.uk@trafford.com

10 9 8 7

CONTENTS

INTRODUCTION:
Understanding What the Torah Really Says

The Torah. The Teaching. The Holy Scroll. The Pentateuch. The Five Books of Moses.

The poet Hayim N. Bialik called it a "mystic, almost cosmetic, conception. The Torah is the tool of the creator; with it and for it he created the universe...it is the highest idea in the living soul of the world."

The Christian scholar Robert T. Herford wrote that the Torah is "[d]ivine teaching upon all and every thing that concerns religion, while Harvard University Biblical Studies Professor George F. Moore called it "[t]he whole content of revelation."[1]

There it sits, in front of just about every Jewish congregation, dressed in its own fitted, embroidered silk cover, with its own gaudy breastplate, inside its own little specially- decorated chamber. When the Ark's door is opened, people rise and murmur in prayer as the scroll is removed. It's so holy that when it's carried around the room, worshipers don't kiss it directly; they kiss their prayer shawls and touch the Torah with them. It's so holy that the reader keeps his place by touching the scroll with a special silver pointer.

In most Jewish congregations, the Torah is read aloud in front of the congregation on the Sabbath and other occasions. Each Jewish boy or girl who has a *bar/bat mitsva* must read a portion of it. I have attended numerous ceremonies in which the youngster gives a stilted speech purporting to explicate a portion of it.

Of course, I say "just about every Jewish congregation" and "most Jewish congregations" because we secular Jewish humanists

---

[1] Definitions are from *The Dictionary of Quotable Definitions* (Englewood Cliffs, NJ: Prentice-Hall Inc.), p. 576.

do not think the Torah deserves all the reverent and obsequious behavior.

It definitely deserves attention. But how much?

This is a very rational question, and for secular humanists, a very natural one. The Torah is an important document, no doubt. So how big a place should it occupy in the Jewish lives and Jewish consciousness of secular humanists? This book will provide an answer.

My basic assumption is a very simple one: humanists can discover for themselves how important the Torah should be to them *by reading the Torah themselves*. They don't need to know Hebrew. They certainly don't have to slog through the arcane and archaic King James Bible. The Jewish Publication Society's third edition, published in 1992, is a magnificent work of scholarship[2] that renders most of the Torah into fully intelligible modern (though hardly colloquial) English.

In other words: you don't have to take anyone's – including a rabbi's – opinion about what is in the Torah. *You can read it for yourself.*

Not that the JPS version is an easy read. It's over 400 pages long. Along with the familiar Sunday school stories, there are many minor characters and lesser plot lines; there are lengthy passages that are nothing but laws, ritual rules, census counts, or genealogy; there's a considerable amount of repetition; and much of the Torah is simply not palatable to modern sensibilities or

---

[2] In the first Appendix to this chapter is some material from the dust jacket and the text of the introduction of the JPS translation. If you read it, you'll be as convinced as I am that it's a truly impressive piece of work.

relevant to modern mores because it was written in and for a vastly different time and place.

On the other hand, secular humanists who are willing to actually read the Torah can arrive at a new sense of understanding - a secular humanistic understanding - of this document, its writers, and the world in which they lived.

The good news is that <u>you</u> don't have to read the Torah - I've done it for you. In this book, I report on what I found.

But, you say, rabbis have been telling me for years what's in the Torah, so why do I need to hear it again?

Because there are two meanings for the phrase "what's in the Torah" - and there's a world of difference between them. What you have heard and read about what's in the Torah...and what the original text actually says (to the extent that scholarship can determine it)...may be two very different things.

One big difference, not very surprising, is that a lot of the Torah's R-rated stuff is never mentioned in Sunday school and rarely if ever discussed from rabbinical pulpits.

I never knew, for example, that after God destroys Sodom and Gomorrah, Lot's two daughters get him drunk and have sex with him because they believe he's the last man in the world and they want to perpetuate their line. I never knew of an incident in which some Israelites, to avenge the rape of their sister, agree to friendship with the rapist's tribe, convince the men to be circumcised, then kill them all while they're recovering from the circumcisions. I never knew about a law in Deuteronomy that prescribes the amputation of a woman's hand if, when two men are fighting, she reaches out to help her husband and grabs his adversary's genitals.

I wonder if Hayim Bialik or Robert Herford read those passages.

The other big difference between the traditional view of the Torah and the actual words of the JPS version is much more important. To give you a concise statement of the view that I'm opposing, I'll quote Joseph Hertz, who for 33 years (beginning in 1913) was Chief Rabbi of Congregation Orach Chayim in New York:

> "The real Torah is not merely the written text of the Five Books of Moses; the real Torah is the meaning enshrined in the text as expounded...and unfolded...by successive generations of sages and teachers in Israel."

That is the perception of many, probably most, Jews: it all started with the Torah. But to me, there's something not quite right about all that expounding and unfolding, even though a great deal of wisdom was developed in the process. [3]

There's a crucial difference – not often recognized – between "what the text says" and "what I say the text says." The latest JPS translation is as authoritative a version as there can be, given the strengths and limitations of modern scholarship, of what the text says. Everything else is what I'll call *inference.*

To a linguist like me, there's a fine, bright line between translation and inference. They are two very different linguistic processes.

---

[3] Wisdom, I hardly need add, that came from cogitating human minds, not external divine inspiration. And there were two other positive results of all the concern with the Torah: the continuation of literacy and the cultivation of a highly verbal, disputatious culture that served Jews well, once the Enlightenment opened up secular opportunities to them.

A ***translation*** is an attempt to reproduce the content – and, to the extent possible the tone, style, and intent – of the source text.

In this regard, the JPS version is a major accomplishment. Yet nearly every page of it has one or more footnotes that provide alternate, sometimes widely differing translations – or simply say "meaning of Heb. uncertain." I mention this because I want you to appreciate how difficult it is to attempt an accurate translation of an ancient text; you may then wonder, as I do, how rabbis can go ahead and make inferences about what the text "means."

An ***inference*** elaborates upon the original. It adds new material. It is a deduction, a conclusion about what the text "really" says, in the opinion of the writer or speaker; it's the filling in of X and Y in the statement that "They couldn't have meant X, so they must have meant Y." An inference purports to know what the writer was thinking. It interprets the text, oftentimes for people who are already quite capable of reading it for themselves.

In my experience, when most lay people and rabbis, with the exception of humanists and serious Bible scholars, talk and write about the Torah, they completely confuse inference with translation. Inference is passed off as "what the Torah teaches." In this book that will not be the case. I deal only with the Torah text. I tell you what it says,[4] and I let you judge for yourself.

The book is divided into chapters as follows:

Chapter I – Reading What the Torah Really Says: Rabbinical Spin at Work. Describes how inference is passed off as Torah text; this is the process by which the

---

[4] In the chapter that summarizes the Torah, all of my comments are in footnotes.

Torah acquires a much better reputation than it deserves.
Chapter II – I Read It (So You Don't Have To). Summarizes the entire content of the Torah, by chapter and verse. You can read it all in an hour or two – and really know what's in the Torah. Then, if you want to read the original, you'll know just where to find it.
Chapter III – Good God!? A portrait of the Torah's main character, based on actual Torah text. It addresses the question of whether God is worthy of our respect.
Chapter IV – How Relevant Is the Torah – Really? I've collected and classified all of the Torah's laws and directives, in an attempt to assess just how much of the Torah is relevant to modern Jewish secular humanists.
Chapter V – Understanding What the Torah Really Says: Why It Matters. Sums up the book and offers a few personal thoughts on the function of religion.

I've been very careful to stay within my limitations. I'm not trained in archaeology, history, Bible studies, or Semitic linguistics. Below, in Appendix II, I provide a brief overview of what people in these disciplines have discovered about who wrote the Torah, when, and why – just enough to provide some background and context.

My main concern is always the text itself.[5] I brought to it

---

[5] In the few places where I really got stuck and didn't know what the text was saying, I consulted Jordan Jay Hillman's book *The Torah and Its God: A Humanist Inquiry* (Amherst, New York: Prometheus Books, 2001). It summarizes the Torah, much as I have done, though with a lot more inference and interpretation. Also, through Hillman's citations, it gave me indirect access to other sources. It is not, in my view, a humanist inquiry, but to fully

no awe, no reverence – just my curiosity, my linguistic expertise, and my sincere desire to know what the Torah really says. Now I know – and so will you.

Appendix I: The Jewish Publication Society Translation

In this Appendix, you'll find background material on the Jewish Publication Society's most recent translation of the Torah. These excerpts should help you understand why the JPS version is such a masterful work of scholarship – and why it is the authoritative modern English translation.

---

explain why would require another entire chapter. Among other things, Hillman is not able, though he strives mightily, to reconcile God's bad behavior with his celestial origins and his supposedly inspiring message for mankind. Also, according to the dust jacket, he "contends that Judaic humanism derives logically from the recognition and acceptance of human origins of the God of the Torah and its God." This is inaccurate: Jewish humanism has several sources, including the ancient prophets and the 18th century Enlightenment, with its monumental consequences for Jews. Moreover, despite Hillman's exhaustive and legalistic commentary, I fail to see how humanism "derives logically" from the mere acceptance of human authorship of the Torah. That in itself is not enough. There must be humanistic content. The Torah does teach some humanistic virtues, but there's more than an equal amount of material that's irrelevant – and in some cases, repugnant – to humanists.

(1) From the dust jacket: General information on the new JPS translation

"The JPS edition of the Torah is an entirely original translation of the Five Books of Moses into contemporary English, based on the Masoretic – the traditional Hebrew – text.

"The new translation is the culmination of three decades of collaboration by scholars and rabbis representing the three largest branches of organized Judaism in America.

"Not since the third century B.C.E., when 72 elders of the tribes of Israel created the Greek translation of scriptures known as the Septuagint, has such a broad-based committee of Jewish scholars produced a major Bible translation.

"In executing this monumental task the translators made use of the entire range of biblical interpretation, ancient and modern, Jewish and non-Jewish. They drew upon the latest findings in linguistics and archaeology, as well as the work of early rabbinic and medieval commentators, Americans, and philologians.

"The resulting text is a triumph of literary style and biblical scholarship, unsurpassed in accuracy and clarity.

"The new JPS translation was originally published in 1962; since then, each edition has been subject to a thorough reexamination of its text. Consequently, while adhering to the same policies and principles of Bible translation that were followed in the first edition, this present edition occasionally differs from it in phrasing and sometimes in meaning."

(2) From the Preface: Why a new translation?

The Preface to the 1962 edition notes that even though the Jewish Publication Society of America produced its first translation of the Bible in 1917, "the need for a new translation has been obvious for years":

> "For one thing it is possible - and therefore necessary - to improve substantially on earlier versions in rendering both the shades of meaning of words and expressions and the force of grammatical forms and constructions. This can be done partly with the help of neglected insights in ancient and medieval Jewish scholarship, and partly by utilizing the new knowledge of the ancient, as well as of the more recent, Near East. For significant advances have been made during the past half-century in biblical archaeology and in the recovery of the languages and civilizations of the people among whom the Israelites lived and whose modes of living and thinking they largely shared. In accuracy alone we believe this translation is vastly improved on the first JPS translation in literally hundreds of passages."

The Preface provides a second reason for creating a new translation: the Bible "must be made intelligible to every generation."

Anyone who thinks the King James Version "is" the Bible should be aware that this version, "upon which almost all English translations of the Bible have hitherto been based, *had an archaic flavor even for its readers in the year 1611, when it was first published* [emphasis mine]. Moreover, it rendered the Hebrew to a considerable extent word for word rather than idiomatically, a procedure which nearly always results in quaintness or awkwardness and not infrequently in obscurity. A translation which is stilted where the original is natural, heavy where the original is graceful, or obscure where the original is perfectly intelligible, is the very opposite of faithful."

Appendix II: Torah FAQs

The last time I checked amazon.com, there were over 6900 books on the Torah. Some of them are scholarly inquiries into the historical, archaeological, anthropological, and linguistic aspects of the Torah. Others are commentary in which the writer makes inferences about what the Torah writers were thinking and what the text "really" means. By the time you've finished reading this book, you'll know which is which.

I encourage you to investigate any aspect of the Torah that interests you (and not to feel guilty if you're not interested). The purpose of this Appendix is simply to provide basic information.

What exactly is the Torah?

(1) *The Torah is not the Talmud; they are completely separate documents*. The Talmud is a vast compilation of the Oral Law (as opposed to Scriptures, i.e., written laws), with rabbinical elucidations, elaborations, and commentaries. The first major part of it, called the Mishna, was originally compiled around 200 C.E.; it contains detailed instructions for following the rules outlined in the Torah.

The Talmud is concerned with many subjects. It contains information and comment on astronomy, geography, historical lore, domestic relations, and folklore. The legal sections of the Talmud are known as the *halakhah*. This is the body of law that regulates all aspects of life – not only religious ritual, but also familial and personal status, civil relations, criminal law, and relations with non-Jews.[6]

(2) *The Torah is not the Bible.* It is the first five of the 24 books of the Hebrew Bible, which Jews call the Tanakh, and Christians and others call The Old Testament.

(3) *The Torah text that you find in synagogues does not come from the time of Moses – or from any ancient era.* It is a copy of a manuscript that dates from 900 C.E. Scholarship tells us that the Torah was assembled in its present form by the fourth century B.C.E., so the earliest assembled version we have dates from 1300 years after the document was first written down. The Dead Sea Scrolls, a thousand years older than the Masoretic text, contain every book of the Torah and seem not to differ significantly. We have no way of knowing exactly what the original Torah says, although we have reason to believe that the ancient text has been fairly well preserved. For more information on the Torah text used in synagogues, see Chapter 1.

If God or Moses didn't write the Torah, who did?

Four different people, according to the Documentary Hypothesis (which to my mind is as well-established as the theories of quantum mechanics or evolution). With one exception, we can't even guess at the authors' names, but we can identify them through their style, and as the result of much painstaking work, we now know that the three of the documents have been interwoven to create the first four books of the Torah.

---

[6] Source for information on the Talmud: encyclopedia.com.

The sources are referred to by letters:[7]

- "E," because the Hebrew word for God in this collection of stories God is "El" or "Elohim";
- "J," for the group of stories in which God is referred to as "Yahweh";
- "P," for the stories that come from a third source, which, as Friedman puts it, "had been hidden within E" and which "seemed to be particularly interested in *priests*." P contains "stories about priests, laws about priests, matters of ritual sacrifice, incense-burning and purity, and concern with dates, numbers, and measurements."

J and E were written by two different people, sometime between 848 and 722 B.C.E. (F87).

Furthermore, the author of J "came from Judah and the author of E came from Israel (F61)." The author of E was "a Shiloh priest who probably thought of Moses as his own ancestor...[because] the E stories offer more development of Moses' personality than those of J – and not just *more* development, but more *sympathetic* development" (F79).

It's possible that the author of J was a woman. In the Judean court, a woman could have had enough status and education to produce such a document. Also, the J stories are "on the whole, much more concerned with women and much more sensitive to women than are the E stories" (F86).

---

[7]The following paragraphs paraphrase Richard Elliott Friedman's *Who Wrote the Bible?* (New York: HarperCollinsPublishers, 1997; hereafter F), pp. 52-53.

And what of the fourth source document? Friedman continues:

> "The sources J, E, and P were found to flow through the first four of the five Books of Moses: Genesis, Exodus, Leviticus, and Numbers. However, there was hardly a trace of them in the fifth book, Deuteronomy, except for a few lines in the last chapters. Deuteronomy is written in an entirely different style from those of the other four books. The differences are obvious even in translation. The vocabulary is different. There are different recurring expressions and favorite phrases. There are doublets of whole sections of the first four books. There are blatant contradictions in detail between it and the others. Even part of the wording of the Ten Commandments is different."

Deuteronomy is thus the work of a fourth, independent writer. Friedman (F125ff.) cites persuasive evidence that it was the prophet Jeremiah.

Jeremiah was also the author of the next five books of the Bible. He "was both a writer and editor." He "lived in Jerusalem around 622 B.C.[E.]" (F116). He "selected the stories and other texts that he wanted to use from sources available to him. He arranged the texts, shortening or adding to them. He inserted occasional comments of his own. And he wrote introductory sentences which he set near the beginning of the work. Overall, he constructed the history that extended from Moses to the destruction of the kingdom of Judah by the Babylonians" (F103).

Who put the various documents together into the Torah?

Despite the fact that the four source documents contain conflicting political statements and points of view, "someone was putting all of these works together." Specifically,

> "Someone was combining JE with [P,] the work that was written as an alternative to it. And this person was not merely combining them side by side, as parallel stories. He...was cutting and intersecting them intricately. And at the end of this combined, interwoven collection of the laws and stories of J, E, and P, this person set Deuteronomy, the farewell speech of Moses, as a conclusion. Someone was merging the four different, often opposing sources so artfully that it would take millennia to figure it out.
>
> "This was the person who created the Torah, the Five Books of Moses that we have read for over 2000 years (F217-8)."

This individual has been known as "the redactor," i.e., the editor. Who was he? According to Friedman, much evidence points convincingly to a Biblical figure named Ezra. Ezra was an Aaronid "priest, scribe, and lawgiver" during the days of the Second Temple (5th century B.C.E). He was an important man who had access to documents. He set out to find the Torah; indeed, the Bible itself, in the Book of Ezra, notes that Ezra "had set his heart on seeking out Yahweh's Torah" (Ezra 7:10). He found it, brought it to Jerusalem, and "personally gave its first public reading" (F223-4).

Of course, no one can be sure that the Torah redactor was in fact Ezra, but if it was not, Friedman contends that "it was someone close to him – a relative, a colleague in the priesthood, a fellow scribe – because [the Torah] could not have been produced very long before he arrived with it in Judah" (F224).

Did any of the events in the Torah actually happen?

In a word, no.

There is no archaeological evidence of anything in the Torah. And in all the ancient writings we've found, there is no record – no mention, in fact – of anything in the Torah. In all of the Egyptians' written records, there's no mention of any Jews in Egypt, no mention of 600,000 of them escaping.

Friedman notes that there are "traditions about the prehistory of the Israelites: their patriarchs, their experience as slaves in Egypt, and their wandering in the Sinai wilderness. Unfortunately, we have little historical information about this from archaeology or other ancient sources. The first point at which we actually have sufficient evidence to begin to picture the life of the Biblical community is the 12th century B.C.E., the period when the Israelites became established in [the Eastern Mediterranean] region" (F35-6).

What about Abraham, Isaac, and Jacob? Finkelstein and Silberman (FS) write in their book *The Bible Unearthed* (New York: Simon and Schuster, 2002) that "the search for the historical patriarchs was ultimately unsuccessful since none of the periods around the biblically suggested date provided a completely compatible background to the Biblical stories" (FS35).

Nor did the Exodus happen in any way remotely resembling the Biblical account. FS observe that "independent archaeological and historical sources tell of migrations of Semites from Canaan to Egypt,[8] and other Egyptians forcibly expelling them. This basic outline of immigration and violent return to Canaan is parallel to the Biblical account of Exodus" (FS56). However, "the Israelites emerged only gradually as a distinct group in Canaan, beginning at the end of the thirteenth century B.C.E. There is no recognizable archaeological evidence of Israelite presence in Egypt immediately

---

[8] For more information, see Eugene Finerman's essay "The Jews in the Ancient World" at the end of Chapter 4 below.

before that time" (FS56).

Also, "the border between Canaan and Egypt was...closely controlled. If a great mass of fleeing Israelites had passed through the border fortifications of the pharaonic regime, a record should exist. Yet in the abundant Egyptian sources describing the time of the New Kingdom in general and the thirteenth century in particular, there is no reference to the Israelites, not even a single clue" (FS59).

FS add that "one can hardly accept the idea of a flight of a large group of slaves from Egypt through the heavily guarded border fortifications into the desert and then into Canaan in the time of such a formidable Egyptian presence. Any group escaping Egypt against the will of the pharaoh would have easily been tracked down not only by Egyptian army chasing from the delta but also by the Egyptian soldiers in the forts in northern Sinai and in Canaan...[Furthermore, t]he possibility of a large group of people wandering in the Sinai Peninsula is also contradicted by archaeology" (FS61).

The inscription on a stone monument from the very end of the thirteenth century B.C.E. "tells of a destructive Egyptian campaign into Canaan, in the course of which a people named Israel were decimated to the extent that the Pharaoh boasted that Israel's 'seed is not!' The boast was clearly an empty one, but it did indicate that some group known as Israel was already in Canaan by that time (FS57)...But we have no clue, not even a single word, about early Israelites *in* Egypt: neither in monumental inscriptions on walls of temples, nor in tomb inscriptions, nor in papyri. Israel is absent – as a possible foe of Egypt, as a friend, or as enslaved nation" (FS59).

Chapter One
Translation and Inference: Understanding the Crucial Difference
Rabbinical Spin at Work: "What the Torah Says" Versus "What I Say It Says"

Introduction: the Torah as a Text

What exactly are we talking about when we refer to "the Torah text"? In the introductory essay of *The Torah: a Modern Commentary,*[9] W. Gunther Plaut provides a concise historical background:

> "There is no original manuscript available which was written by any of the authors of the Bible. The oldest extant parchment scroll of the Torah dates from about 900 C.E., which is probably more than 1300 years later than the likely time of its composition. Quite naturally, much happens to a text in the course of oral transmission and copying by hand and one must not be astonished that a number of variances in versions arose. It is a great tribute to the care and devotion which were lavished on the text that the variants are relatively minor and the scribal corruptions rather few. Our commentary uses the Masoretic version. The Masoretes, so called because they transmitted the *Masorah* (מסורה) or textual traditions, were scholars who over the centuries attempted to ascertain and preserve the best text. One of these versions, produced in Tiberius in the 10th century C.E., found general acceptance and is the standard Hebrew text in synagogue use today."

---

[9] New York: Union of American Hebrew Congregations, 1981.

Plaut notes that as knowledge of classical Hebrew declined, the Torah was translated into Aramaic (the popular language of postexilic Jews), Greek, Latin, and eventually into every written language of modern times. He adds:

> "The important ancient translations often give us significant clues about the original from which they were translated, for there are differences between them. What is even more important is to recognize that every translator interprets the original text, for he renders it as he understands (or misunderstands) it."

Plaut observes that are significant differences among the various modern translations and says that

> "[m]any of these differences are stylistic since the language of translation has itself undergone vast changes;[10] others are due to new insights into the philology[11] of ancient days and political of social, and economic circumstances to which the text refers."

Which translation does the exhaustive *Modern Commentary* use? Why, that of the Jewish Publication Society, of course. Plaut writes that

> " [t]his translation, in addition to its scholarly and linguistic merits, has been made particularly valuable by the publication of the translators' *Notes on the New Translation of the Torah*...which explains in detail why certain translations

---

[10] For example, the King James and the later American versions, both in English yet quite different from each other.

[11] Philology is the study of language origins, interrelationships, and change, especially the history of individual words and phrases; its data typically consists of written texts from earlier times.

were chosen and others rejected."

So, to sum it up: When I tell you what's in "the Torah," my comments are based on a highly refined and many-times revised (yet inevitably inaccurate) English translation of a 10th century Hebrew text that is the result of thirteen centuries of copying the original Torah. It's as close as we can come. There's no way to know what the original Torah said.

Ways of Transforming the Torah Text: Translation, Inference, Paraphrase, Commentary – and Rabbinical Spin

The central premise of this book is that ***there is a significant difference between "what the Torah says" and "what I say the Torah says," between translation and inference***. In the Introduction, I explained that difference. In this chapter, I'll give you a detailed example of it.

As a linguist – and a longtime observer of how language is used – I've noted that congregants, rabbis, and in fact most if not all Jewish believers act as if there is no difference whatsoever. In almost all Jewish congregations, in almost all talk and writing about the Torah, the difference between translation and inference is completely ignored. The two are routinely intermingled and confused.

Thus there is no way readers or listeners who have not read the Torah can tell whether they're getting a paraphrase[12] of a Torah passage, an interpretation of it, an elaboration of it, or any of several kinds of inferences about it.

---

[12] To paraphrase is to express the same content – and only the same content – in different words. Whenever I tell you what the Torah says, I'm always paraphrasing, never inferring. My opinions about the Torah are clearly labeled as such.

Let me unambiguously state that I have no objection to such intellectual pastimes as positing metaphors and allegories, identifying universal themes, or constructing and comparing opinions about what the writer(s) of the original text "really meant." If rabbis and Torah scholars want to find meanings within meanings within meanings, that's fine with me.

Literature professors and literary critics do the same. But academics and critics make a clear distinction between "what the text says," on the one hand, and, on the other, "what I say the text says" or "what the text means **to me**." They distinguish between (a) the actual text that they're interpreting and (b) the interpretation itself.

But when rabbis (and other clerics too, because my point applies to the entire Bible and other sacred texts as well) fail to make this distinction, they're not being honest with their audiences. By passing off their inferences and interpretations as Torah content,[13] they can make the document seem much more benevolent and relevant than it is.

In this chapter, I want to demonstrate, with actual examples and Torah text, the difference between "what it says" and "what I say it says."

In this case, the person asserting that "the Torah says what I say it says" is Rabbi Arthur Waskow, who directs the Shalom Center in Philadelphia. I will be quoting from "Reclaiming Our Day of Rest: Why We Should Keep the Sabbath," an article that Rabbi Waskow wrote for the January-February 2004 Issue of *The Utne Reader*.

---

[13] Other techniques include selective quotation and quoting out of context; both are illustrated in this chapter.

Rabbi Waskow is, to quote from the bio at the end of his article, "one of the pioneers of the Jewish Renewal movement, which seeks to bring traditional Jewish spirituality into relationship with contemporary currents such as feminism and environmentalism."

I have the greatest respect and good will for Rabbi Waskow and his fine work. And I emphatically agree with his position on the importance of resting on the Sabbath. All I'm concerned with here is the difference between (a) what the Torah says and (b) what he says it says.

The Rabbi cites six Torah passages. In this chapter, I'll compare what he says with the JPS text, citation by citation.

(1) Exodus 20:8-11
From the Rabbi's article:
"For all the religious traditions that take the Hebrew Scriptures seriously, there is a teaching we call *Shabbat*. The word, usually translated into English as Sabbath, comes from the Hebrew verb for pausing or ceasing. In Exodus 20:8-11, the reason given for the Sabbath is to recall Creation;..."

Corresponding Torah passage:
Exodus 20:8-11 – "Remember the Sabbath day and keep it only. Six days you shall labor and do your work, but the seventh day is a Sabbath of the Lord your God: you shall not do any work – you, your son or daughter, your male or female slaves, or your cattle, or the stranger who is within your settlements. For in six days the Lord made heaven and earth and sea, and all that is in them, and He rested on the seventh day; therefore the Lord blessed the Sabbath day and

hallowed it."

My evaluation: In this case the Rabbi accurately reports the content of the Torah text.

(2) Deuteronomy 5:12-15
From the Rabbi's article:
"... in Deuteronomy 5:12-15, [the reason given for observing the Sabbath] is to free all of us from slavery."

Corresponding Torah passage:
Deuteronomy 5:12-15 – "Observe the Sabbath day and keep it holy, as the Lord your God has commanded you. Six days you shall labor and do all your work, but the seventh day is a Sabbath of the Lord your God; you shall not do any work – you, your son or your daughter, your male or female slaves, your ox or your ass, or any of your cattle, or the stranger in your settlements, so that your male and female slaves may rest as you do. Remember that you were slaves in the land of Egypt and the Lord your God freed you from there with a mighty hand and an outstretched arm; therefore the Lord your God has commanded you to observe the Sabbath day."

My evaluation: Here Rabbi Waskow is spinning. He deviates from the Hebrew text, which simply tells people to observe the Sabbath <u>because</u> God rescued them from slavery; observing the Sabbath is a way of remembering their deliverance.

That is a very different proposition from "to free all of us from slavery." The Torah did <u>not</u> say something like

"...Remember that work can be like slavery; therefore, one day each week you shall free yourselves from this obligation and enjoy your freedom."

The Rabbi is not just paraphrasing now; he has changed the meaning of the original.

Now let's consider the Rabbi's other four citations:

(3) Leviticus 25
(4) Leviticus 26:34-35
(5) Leviticus 26:43-45
(6) Deuteronomy 15:1-18

In his article, these all occur in one place – right after the sentence that begins with the words "All land was redistributed..." – even though the content of the passages themselves covers many other subjects than that one sentence.

By citing all four at once, he follows a quasi-academic convention – that what he says is somehow a summary or paraphrase of all four (in this case, it isn't).

Here's the whole quote from Rabbi Waskow:

"And we are taught not only the seven-day Shabbat: There are also the seventh year (still present in our time in the form of the sabbatical) and the seven-times-seven-plus-one year (the 50th year or Jubilee).

"In the seventh year, the land must be allowed to catch its breath and rest, to make a Shabbat for God, the Breath of Life. Since nearly everyone in ancient Israel was a shepherd or farmer, this meant that almost the whole society rested. Since no one was getting orders and no one was obeying them, hierarchies of bosses and workers vanished. In this yearlong Shabbat, even debt – a form of stored-up hierarchy – was unknown. Those who have been forced to borrow money because of poverty were released from the need to repay; those who had been pressed into lending their wealth were released from the need to collect."

"In this 50th year, the land was not worked so it could breathe freely once again. All land was redistributed in equally productive shares, clan by clan, as it had originally been held **(Leviticus 25 and 26:34-35, 43-45; Deuteronomy 15:1-18)**. These yearlong jubilee observances that the Bible calls *shabbat shabbatom*, ("Sabbath to the Sabbatical power" or "deeply restful rest") are times for enacting social justice and freeing the earth from human exploitation. They are times of release from attachments and habits, addictions and idolatries."

Those are all the Torah passages that the Rabbi cites. Now let's go back through his article and see how well his statements[14] match up against what the text actually says. As you'll see, the Rabbi's statements about what the Torah says are partly accurate, partly not. Paraphrase and inference are freely mixed.

- **From the article:**
  "In the seventh year, the land must be allowed to catch its breath and rest, to make a Shabbat for God, the Breath of Life."

---

[14] Discounting the first one (about the modern sabbatical), which is not a comment on what the Torah says.

Corresponding Torah passage:
D25:4 – "But in the seventh year the land shall have a Sabbath of complete rest, a Sabbath of the Lord: you shall not sow your field or prune your vineyard."
My evaluation: The Rabbi's statements are mostly a paraphrase of Torah text; however, the references to "catch its breath" and "a Shabbat for God, the Breath of Life" are not in the Torah text. Notice how paraphrase and metaphorical inference are mingled in a single sentence.

- **From the article:**
"Since nearly everyone in ancient Israel was a shepherd or farmer, this meant that almost the whole society rested. Since no one was getting orders and no one was obeying them, hierarchies of bosses and workers vanished."

Corresponding Torah passage:
There is nothing in the Torah text that corresponds to any of this!

My evaluation: Both statements – that "the whole society rested" and that "whole hierarchies of bosses and workers vanished" – are inferences about what happened as a result of following the Torah's commandments.

Such inferences may be supported by historical or archaeological evidence, but the Rabbi cites none. That's not surprising: the Israelites were not important enough to rate more than rare mention in the texts from other contemporaneous groups, and there was no other independent internal source of information about them – the Torah was the first. The Rabbi's first inference – that everybody rested – is pretty logical, but the second represents quite a stretch. Who knows whether hierarchies disappeared? In any event, neither corresponds in any way to Torah text.

- **From the article:**
  "In this yearlong Shabbat, even debt – a form of stored-up hierarchy – was unknown. Those who had been forced to borrow money because of poverty were released from the need to repay; those who had been pressed into lending their wealth were released from the need to collect."

  Corresponding Torah passages:
  Leviticus 25:25 – "If your kinsman is in straits and has to sell part of his holding, his nearest redeemer[15] shall come and redeem what his kinsman has sold...If he lacks sufficient means to recover it, what he sold shall remain with the purchaser until the jubilee; in the jubilee year it shall be released, and he shall return to his holding."

  Deuteronomy 15:1-3 – "Every seventh year you shall

[15] Also translated by JPS "a fellow Israelite" (p. 238, note *c*).

practice remission of debts. This shall be the nature of the remission: every creditor shall remit the due that he claims from his fellow; he shall not dun his fellow or kinsman, for the remission proclaimed is of the Lord. You may dun the foreigner; but you must remit whatever is due you from your kinsman."

My evaluation: The Rabbi is accurately paraphrasing and summarizing the Torah text, with one notable exception: the phrase "a form of stored-up hierarchy." This is a modern interpretation with no corresponding Torah text: who really knows whether or not the ancient Israelites considered debt a form of stored-up hierarchy?

- **From the article:**
  "In this 50th year, the land was not worked so it could breathe freely once again."

  Corresponding Torah passage:
  Deuteronomy 25:4 – "But in the seventh year the land shall have a Sabbath of complete rest, a Sabbath of the Lord: you shall not sow your field or prune your vineyard."

  My evaluation:
  This sentence begins with a paraphrase of the Torah text ("In this 50th year, the land was not worked...") and ends with a literary extrapolation ("...so it could breathe freely once again").

- **From the article:**
  "All land was redistributed in equally productive shares, clan by clan, as it had originally been held..."

  Corresponding Torah passage (?):
  Leviticus 25:13 – "In this year of jubilee, each of you shall return to his holding."

  My evaluation:
  I could not find anything in the passages that the Rabbi cites that corresponds to his statement. The closest I found was N33:54 – a passage about what the Israelites are to do with conquered land! There's nothing in that passage about "equally productive shares."

- **From the article:**
  "These yearlong Jubilee observances that the Bible calls *shabbat shabbatom*, ('Sabbath to the Sabbatical power' or 'deeply restful rest') are times for enacting social justice and freeing the earth from human exploitation. They are times of release from attachments and habits, addictions and idolatries."

  Corresponding Torah passage:
  Leviticus 25:4 – "But in the seventh year the land shall have a Sabbath of complete rest ..."

  My evaluation:
  The only piece of this that has anything

corresponding to it in the JPS translation of the Torah (other than the phrase "year-long Jubilee observances") is the mention of *shabbat shabbatom,* which the JPS translates as "a Sabbath of complete rest."

The remainder is complete invention – a total departure from the Torah text. It may reflect the multiple overlay of generations of commentators commenting on commentators. Or it may be the Rabbi's own politico-religious take on the Torah. *But the original document says absolutely nothing* about "social justice,"[16] "freeing the earth from human exploitation," or "release from attachments and habits, addictions and idolatries."

But we're not done yet. And neither is Rabbi Waskow. I've noted the places where his statements are backed by Torah text, some of which is in the passages he cites. But there's more in these passages than the Rabbi lets on.

Let's go back to the last three passages he cites:

(4) Leviticus 26:34-35

(5) Leviticus 26:43-45

(6) Deuteronomy 15:1-18[17]

---

[16] Unless one counts D15:7-10 – "If there is a needy person among you, you must be generous to him, even if the year of remission is approaching." But the definition of "social justice" changes over time, as evidenced by the fact that other material in the very passages that the Rabbi cites deals with the treatment of slaves.

[17] The Rabbi's other citation – Leviticus 25 – (too lengthy to repeat here) consists entirely of laws and regulations regarding the jubilee. The

First, I'll consider the two quotes from Leviticus.

In my opinion, Leviticus 26 is one of the most passionate chapters in the Torah. It is a long and elaborate litany of the ills and misfortunes that will befall the Israelites if they stray from God's commandments (e.g., if they become secular humanists).

In this chapter the writer's fervid creativity depicts punishments of exquisite horror and misery, as awful as anything envisioned by Jonathan Edwards or Stephen King. A sample: "I will wreak misery upon you – consumption and fever, which cause the eyes to pine and the body to languish; you shall sow your seed to no purpose, for your enemy shall eat it... I will break your proud glory. I will make your skies like iron and your earth like copper, so that your strength shall be spent to no purpose...You shall eat the flesh of your sons and the flesh of your daughters. I will destroy your cult places and cut down your incense stands, and I will heap your carcasses upon your lifeless fetishes."

Now, in this context of these threats, we find the two passages that the Rabbi cites:

> L26:34-35 – "Then shall the land make up for its sabbath years throughout the time that it is desolate and you are the land of your enemies; then shall the land rest and make up for its sabbath years. Throughout the time that it is desolate, it shall observe the rest it did not observe in your sabbath years while you were dwelling upon it."
>
> L26:43-45 – "For the land shall be forsaken of them, making up for its sabbath years by being desolate of them, while they atone for their iniquity; for the abundant reason that they rejected My rules and spurned My laws. Yet, even then

---

directives are much more legalistic than idealistic.

when they are in the land of their enemies, I will not reject them or spurn them so as to destroy them, annulling my covenant with them: for I the Lord am their God. I will remember in their favor the covenant with the ancients, whom I freed from the land of Egypt in the sight of the nations to be their God: I, the Lord."

I cannot emphasize this strongly enough: *in the context of Leviticus, Chapter 26, these are not injunctions or directives to let the land rest and lie fallow; they are threats.* They tell us what will happen if the Israelites stray from God's law.

In addition, in the second passage, L25:43-45 (here I'm paraphrasing, of course), God says that he's not going to do away with the Israelites entirely, for that would annul his covenant; his reasoning is that you can't have a covenant if one of the parties is dead.

The Rabbi has given us a classic example of how one can warp the intended meaning of a Torah passage by taking it out of context. Part of the implied meaning of a sentence is the purpose that it serves: what is the speaker or writer trying to accomplish by creating this particular utterance? Taking quotes out of context ignores this important element of meaning.

Finally, **Deuteronomy 15:1-18**. Here's a synopsis:

D15:1-3 – Instructions to practice, every seventh year, forgiveness of debts. "You may dun the foreigner; but you must remit whatever is due you from your kinsman."

D15:4-5 – If you only heed the Lord, there will be no needy among you.

D15:6 – "For the Lord your God will bless you as he has promised you: you will extend loans to many nations, but require none yourself; you will dominate many nations, but they will not dominate you."[18]

D15:7-11 – If there is a needy person among you, you must be generous to him, even if the year of remission is approaching.

D15:10 – "Give to him readily and have no regrets when you do so for in return the Lord your God will bless you in all your efforts and other undertakings. D15:11 – For there will never cease to be needy ones in your land, which is why I command you, open your hand to the poor and needy kinsman in your land."

D15:12-18 – Rules for freeing one's slaves. D15:16-17 – If the slave wants to remain in your household, "you shall take an awl and put it through his ear into the door, and he shall become your slave in perpetuity."

These passages contain a wide variety of commandments that reflect the moral sophistication of the ancient Israelites. The Torah tells people to take care of the needy - then follows that with instructions about sticking an awl through your slave's ear into the door.

The passage does mention the forgiveness of debts. The forgiveness is limited: you may dun the foreigner, but not your kinsman. Most of the rest of it is irrelevant to the Rabbi's point.

In addition – and once again, let me emphasize this – ***these passages from Deuteronomy say nothing whatsoever about "enacting social justice and freeing the earth from human exploitation" or "release from attachments and habits, addictions and idolatries." Those are modern concepts which have been***

---

[18]A passage that is both eerily prophetic and easily used as a justification for anti–Semitism.

overlaid upon the simple morality of the Torah.

But the Rabbi isn't finished yet either. He has much more to tell us about what the Torah says:

> "Indeed, in these socially revolutionary passages of Torah, the text never uses the word *tzedek* – justice – but instead the words *shmitah* and *dror*, which mean "release," what Buddhists today call nonattachment. The deepest root of social justice, according to these Biblical passages, is the profoundly restful experience of abandoning control over others and over the earth."

Regarding the first sentence and the accuracy of Rabbi Waskow's translation:

A translation is an attempt to the remove the language barrier, to make the source text speak to us as the writer intended, in terms we can understand. It's hard enough to translate contemporary texts of well-known languages – and much harder to translate ancient texts of languages no longer spoken.

Any guess about what a word meant to the person who wrote it in the 10th century (that's 1,300 years and who-knows-how-many hand-copied editions after the original) is just that: a guess. *Shmitah* and *dror* equal nonattachment? Who knows? The Rabbi is making a huge philosophical and semantic leap of faith.

His second sentence *may* be true (or at least arguable) without the phrase "according to these Biblical passages." But as it stands, it is simply not true of the Torah text, which - I hardly need point out - says nothing about "social justice," let alone its "deepest root" or "the profoundly restful experience of abandoning control over others and over the earth." Furthermore, the ideas in the Torah passage are "socially revolutionary" only in the sense that forgiveness of debts and letting the land rest were evidently new concepts in ancient Israelite society. They may or may not be good ideas today.

More important, though, is the confusion that the Rabbi creates when he follows the phrase "socially revolutionary" with a misstatement of what the Torah says. We are led to believe that the Torah contains sophisticated, "socially revolutionary" ideas like nonattachment and abandonment of control. It does not.

Some[19] of the Elements of Rabbinical Spin

Now that you've seen rabbinical spin at work, let me summarize some of the various aspects of it. Note that just a few paragraphs of one person's Torah commentary can contain a number of different spin strategies.

Rabbinical spin consists of the following linguistic devices and processes:

- *Inaccurate paraphrasing of Torah text to alter the original meaning.*

  Example:
  In his discussion of Deuteronomy 5:12-15, Rabbi Waskow says that the reason given for observing the Sabbath is "to free all of us from slavery." But the text tells people to observe the Sabbath *because* God rescued them from slavery; observing the Sabbath is a way of remembering their deliverance. The Torah says nothing about whether or not the purpose of the Sabbath is to free us from slavery.

---

[19] I say "some" because I'm pretty sure that if I examined even a moderate amount of Torah commentary, I would find others.

- *Mixing paraphrase with metaphorical inference, thus giving the impression that* *__both__* *represent Torah text.*

  Examples:
  (a) "In the seventh year, the land must be allowed to **catch its breath** and rest, to make a Shabbat **for God, the Breath of Life**."
  (b) "In this yearlong Shabbat, even debt – **a form of stored-up hierarchy** – was unknown.
  (c) "In this 50th year, the land was not worked **so it could breathe freely once again**."

  The boldfaced phrases do not paraphrase or summarize anything in the Torah text. They represent the Rabbi's metaphorical inferences.

- *Mixing paraphrase of Torah text with inferences about the supposed positive consequences, in ancient Israel, of following the Torah's Commandments.*

  Example:
  "In the seventh year, the land must be allowed to catch its breath and rest, to make a Shabbat for God, the Breath of Life. Since nearly everyone in ancient Israel was a shepherd or farmer, this meant that almost the whole society rested. Since no one was getting orders and no one was obeying them, hierarchies of bosses and workers vanished."

  There is nothing about either of the last two

sentences in the six Torah passages that the Rabbi cites – or anywhere in the Torah. By subtly merging Torah paraphrase with an imaginary "this is how it must have been," he describes positive outcomes of Torah commandments as if he'd been there. He was not.

- *Taking Torah passages out of context, thereby making them seem to mean what they do not.*

Examples:
Leviticus 26:34-35 and 43-45. In context, these passages have nothing to do with either the people or the land resting on the Sabbath. They are threats about what will happen to the Israelites if they do not follow God's law.

- *Making unsupported semantic inferences and philosophical leaps across eras and cultures.*

Example:
"...the words *shmitah* and *dror*, which mean 'release,' what Buddhists today call nonattachment."

- *Outright invention of material that does not correspond to anything in the Torah.*

Examples:
(a) "These yearlong Jubilee observances...are times for enacting social justice and freeing the earth from human exploitation. They are times of release from

attachments and habits, addictions and idolatries."

There is nothing about any of this in the six Torah passages – or anywhere in the JPS version of the Torah.

(b) "The deepest root of social justice, according to these Biblical passages, is the profoundly restful experience of abandoning control over others and over the earth."

There is nothing about any of this in the six Torah passages – or anywhere in the JPS version of the Torah.

I hope that by this point I have imbued you with a healthy skepticism about what someone tells you "the Torah says." As W. Gunther Plaut writes,

> "[The distinction between] what the Torah actually said or meant to say and...what it was believed to have said and to have meant...is important, for in reading the Torah one should keep in mind that what the authors said in their own time to their own contemporaries within their own intellectual framework is one thing and what later generations did with this text, what they contributed to it by commentary and homily, is another" (p. xix).

Not all commentary is spin.

I have no objection to Torah commentary that actually explains what the Torah says. In the Introduction I said that the JPS translates most of the Torah into intelligible modern English. But some of it is not fully intelligible.

There are many words and phrases for which alternate translations are possible - and quite a few for which no definitive translation is possible.

In other cases the Torah text is accurately translated but not fully understandable to the lay reader. For example, the Torah contains several references to "cult prostitutes." Most modern readers would not know that these are women who perform sex in association with fertility and other cults, as opposed to common harlots.

For secular humanists who want a more accurate understanding of what the Torah says, these kinds of commentary are very useful.

But when speakers and writers insert their own metaphors and inferences into the same sentences that supposedly paraphrase Torah text; when they paraphrase inaccurately and thus change the meaning of the original; when they take passages out of context and thereby change their meaning; when they make long metaphorical and philosophical leaps across eons and cultures; when they make up things that are not in the Torah and then either imply or say outright that those things <u>are</u> in the Torah, thus pretending (and persuading other Jews to believe) that the Torah says what it does not say...they are practicing ***rabbinical spin***.

Rabbinical spin is not only confusing and misleading. It is soothing and hypnotic. It fills us with warm, benign feelings for the holy scroll, for the rabbi's erudition, for the whole magnificent edifice of commentary built upon commentary.

A Secular Humanist's Truth

Rabbinical spin leads us away from a secular humanist's truth about the Torah: that it is an ancient text reflecting primitive ways and primitive morals; that it was written by human beings for purposes that were religious, philosophical, and political – and perhaps for other reasons as well; that it is an important source of information about our ancestors and their world; and that, perhaps most important of all, it has little or nothing new to say to contemporary Jews about how to live their lives.

In Chapter Four, I identify everything in the Torah that's relevant to us - on the basis of what the Torah actually says. It can be boiled down to about 30 imprecations that will come as news to no one.

It is rabbinical spin, and rabbinical spin alone, that gives the Torah its contemporary relevance. Generally speaking, if a rabbi or scholar believes in God, he or she will practice rabbinical spin (although I know of one purportedly humanist rabbi who does it).

Thus W. Gunther Plaut, whom I quoted earlier as being fully aware of the difference between text and commentary, nevertheless says, on the same page that I cited, that

> "The Torah is ancient Israel's distinctive record of its search for God. It attempts to record the meeting of the human and Divine, the great moments of the encounter. Therefore, the text is often touched by the ineffable Presence. The Torah tradition testifies to a people of extraordinary spiritual sensitivity. God is not the author of the text, the people are; but God's voice may be heard through theirs if we listen with open minds."

I read the Torah too, and my reaction is: "What is he talking about?"

After you have read this book, you will be able to evaluate for yourself the accuracy of Plaut's statements. You may come to the same conclusion as I have: that people who can make the leap of faith and believe in God can also make the same leap with regard to the Torah. They convince themselves that "it testifies to a people of extraordinary spiritual sensitivity," through whom "God's voice may be heard," and thus is worthy of all sorts of intellectual elaboration – in fact, needful of such elaboration. They assume that "it can't mean X, so it must mean Y." They twist it and spin it until it is indeed relevant and profound.

If one is inclined to find deeper meaning in almost anything[20] and looks hard enough for it, one will find it, in abundance. And what one finds will be conditioned by one's cultural context and social sensibilities.

Thus Plaut notes that "passages with which held little or minor meaning in the past now speak to us suddenly with urgent voice. For instance, the story of Babel was for many years seen as a tale of human arrogance; today it speaks to us as a warning about the dehumanizing effects of urban life."[21]

If one already believes that humans are insignificant insects in the divine scheme of things, then one will certainly read arrogance into the Babel story. If one is already inclined toward negative sociological judgments about cities, one will see "a warning about the dehumanizing effects of urban life."

What if we read what the Torah actually says? Genesis 11:5-6 tells us that God took a look at "the city and tower that man built, and...said, 'If as one people with one language for all, this is how they have begun to act, then nothing that they may propose to do will be out of their reach." That's when God decides to "confound" their languages.

---

[20] I am reminded of an episode of *Star Trek* ("A Piece of the Action") in which the Enterprise comes upon a race of highly imitative beings who have based their entire culture on a book about gangs in Chicago in the 1920s.

[21] *Ibid.*

As a linguist, I can tell you that God's reasoning is correct: one of the major impediments to human progress is the existence of language barriers. As a humanist, I read the Torah text, and it tells me that the writer is not very enthusiastic about human aspirations.

Conclusion: Some Comments on "Literalism"

My approach to the Torah text and its contents will no doubt be derided by many Jews, as well as non-Jewish Bible enthusiasts, as "too literal." W. Gunther Plaut is one of those anti-literalists. He writes:

> "Contemporary readers are often put off because they have been exposed to a method of biblical interpretation which understands the text in a literal way. Thus, if Genesis says that God created woman out of the rib of man, or tells of a serpent speaking, or of ancient man living several hundred years, the literalist interprets the story to mean precisely what the words convey. This literal application reaches down to individual words and phrases.
>
> "Quite aside from the indisputable fact that the Torah text we use today is merely one available version (although the accepted one) and aside from the fact that most literalists not knowing the Hebrew original base their opinions on one particular translation (which is in itself a type of interpretation and therefore a secondary source), the contemporary reader familiar with the history and nature of the text will have to remember that literal understanding of the Torah may lead to grave misconceptions.[22]
>
> "Even the ancient the Jewish Sages, who believed

[22] What "grave misconceptions"? He never says.

> that the Torah was a divinely authored book, did not take the text literally. They took it seriously, but they always looked behind the flat literal meaning. They realized that the Bible – in addition to everything else that it was to them – abounded in subtle metaphors and allusions, that it used wordplay and other literary devices, that it sometimes spoke satirically, and that its poetry could not be subjected to a simple approach" (p. xx).

Plaut (and others who believe the way he does, which is just about everybody) is shooting at a straw-man literalism and ignoring another kind.

Their World – Not Ours

When it comes to understanding what the Torah says, humanists actually start from the same point as Orthodox Jews: I agree with the most ardent fundamentalist that the Torah means exactly what it says.

But the humanist quickly diverges from the fundamentalist: the Torah text is an honest expression of our ancestors' world view - but not of ours.

Furthermore, as believers in science and reason, we know that the Torah writers meant exactly what they said *to the extent that we can determine it.*

Any translation of an ancient text represents only the consensus of human observers. The final product will be pretty accurate, perhaps even largely accurate in places (we'll never really know), but riddled with inaccuracies and question marks.

The humanist accepts the Torah for what it is. Humanists know that we're working from a thousand-year-old text that represents 1,300 years of copying the original. It's not difficult for humanists to live with the Torah's indeterminacy, its inconsistencies - or, for that matter, its violations of the laws of physics and its primitive mores.

I think it's hard for fundamentalists to live with this kind of dissonance. The fundamentalist adopts some version – King James, JPS, Masoretic text, translation into language *x* in the year *y*; it doesn't matter which – and takes it literally.

But what about all the material that is repugnant to modern sensibilities? What about all the passages of whose meaning we can never be certain?

Fundamentalists work hard to answer these questions. Many of them believe that "if your thinking and science don't jibe with the Torah, then there's something wrong with your thinking, your science, or your interpretation of the Torah."

Humanists can live with these questions quite easily. They simply answer that the Torah is what it is.

The kind of literalism that concerns Plaut is that of Orthodoxy: the belief that if the Torah says that a serpent spoke, then it spoke.

But I am not one of those "contemporary readers" who are "put off" by a literal reading of the Torah. No, I don't believe that a snake could speak. But there is a wide range of secular humanist positions on talking snakes – positions that are compatible with reason, human dignity, and what we know about language, anthropology, and literature.

Perhaps the writer him/herself believed that God could make serpents speak, even though he/she had never witnessed it. Perhaps the story was handed down as a fable from time immemorial. Perhaps somebody originally thought of it in a dream or a vision and spread it around the tribe. In those times, the conventional boundary between reality and unreality wasn't where it is today.

Those just a few possibilities that occur to me. I'm sure you can come up with your own.

But that's not enough for many modern, educated Jews in Israel, in Europe, in North America, and elsewhere. They want some sort of intellectually nice-sounding middle position. They want to cling to tradition, but in a way that they can accept.

Liberal Rabbis to the Rescue!

Here's where the non-Orthodox rabbis come in. They are a bridge between the doctrine of the fundamentalists and the needs of moderns, who, for example, cannot merely accept the Torah's anti-feminist bias – they somehow have to *reconcile* the Torah with feminism. Rabbinical spin to the rescue!

Liberal rabbis trade in making the unpalatable palatable, through all the devices I've laid out in this chapter and no doubt more besides.

In general, I've noticed that the more liberal the cleric, the thicker the spin. There are more metaphors and allegories – and less talk about the Torah's mind-numbing rituals and rules, its many death penalties, God's grotesque threats to and violent punishments upon the Israelites, and so on.

No humanist is the kind of literalist that Plaut criticizes. No humanist believes that a serpent spoke or that a man lived nine centuries. But in the world of the Torah – or the Torah writer's imagination – that's the way it happened. That's what our ancestors believed.

Literalism and Science

The kind of literalism that I espouse is one that Plaut appears to be unaware of: the literalism that is backed by reason and science. Of course, the JPS translation is a consensus and to some extent a conjecture, but unlike rabbinical spin, it is not the product of selective quoting, or of quoting out of context, or of saying, "God actually meant..." – or of just making things up.

It is the result of many decades of hard, exacting analysis of countless pieces of specific language data to discover such key phenomena as the multiple authorship and synoptic editing of the Torah – and then, over more decades, to render the sense of the original into many languages, including modern English.

Before people knew these scientific methods, they spent centuries debating whether or not Moses had written the Torah.

The JPS translation is the result of countless scholar-hours invested in developing and defending hypothesis after hypothesis about how each word and passage should be translated.

The documentary theory about the authorship and synoptic editing of the Torah – as soundly established, in my opinion, as the theories of evolution or general relativity – was a similar detective story, involving hypothesis after hypothesis, supported then refuted by data and analysis, then supplanted by another hypothesis. As in any other scientific endeavor, the truth with which we are concerned - the truth of what the Torah actually says - is elusive but approachable.

The literalism in which the humanist believes is based on reason and science - in this case linguistics, with help from anthropology, history, archaeology, and other disciplines.

To a humanist, the Torah says what it says. And what the Torah says is the sum of...

- its semantics (what each word, phrase and idiom

means),[23]

- its syntax (the relationships between its words and phrases; the relationship of one sentence to another);
- and its pragmatics (what the writer of a particular passage is trying to accomplish, e.g., instruct, dictate behavior, threaten, promise, achieve a political goal by selecting events and/or narrating them in a particular way).

This approach does accommodate puns, wordplay, poetry, and satire. It may be possible to tell when a Torah writer is practicing these (I didn't find any satire). For instance, many names, according to the text itself, are based on events or items associated with the individuals so named.

But commentators freely and frequently depart from the text. To me, the relevant questions are: How directly can a particular metaphor or wordplay be deduced from the text or its context? How much could be <u>independently deduced by another individual?</u> How much is imagined or invented?

Remember, if one is predisposed to find the Torah profound, one will (much as one might find a child's first words precious). I was not and did not.

Communication consists of the above three types of information. If we can get all three from an ancient text, we're doing well: we have a reliable idea of what the writer intended to say. Insofar as we can understand what the Torah writers were trying to communicate at all three of the above levels,[24] we can

---

[23] These are informal definitions.

[24] With the help of external information, of course, such as in the example of "cult prostitutes."

come to some sort of understanding of what they wrote.

That is translation. Everything else is inference.

Chapter Two
I Read It (So You Don't Have To)

A Summary of the Torah's Content

In this chapter I summarize the entire Torah, by chapter and verse, with absolutely no interpretation or spin (all of my comments are in footnotes). The amount of detail that I use for a particular chapter depends in most cases on how interesting the material is likely to be to a modern secular reader who simply wants to know what the Torah says. Thus, if an entire chapter consists of nothing but rituals, genealogy, or census counts, I note that fact and move on.

Where there is narrative, I summarize events fairly closely. If any verse is left out or unaccounted for, it is for one of two reasons: either the material is just elaboration of a particular topic (e.g., additional laws covering the behavior of the priests or the observance of a holiday), or it is repetitive and low-content, as with the passages that say that the Israelites go off and do that which God or Moses has commanded.

I've used boldfaced type to identify familiar Bible stories and events. Enjoy.

GENESIS

Genesis, Chapter 1

God creates the world. First he separates light from darkness, then the sky from the water, then the water from dry land. He then creates plants, animals, man, and woman, in that order.

Genesis, Chapter 2

This chapter - the first of many "doublets" that indicate multiple authorship - starts over with a different version of creation. God creates man first, then plants, then, to keep the man from being lonely, animals. Finally, since there was "no fitting helper" for Adam among the animals, God creates woman.

G2:17 – God tells Adam that he can eat of every tree in the garden, "but as for the tree of knowledge of good and bad, you must not eat of it; for as soon as you eat of it, you shall die."

Genesis, Chapter 3

The serpent, "the shrewdest of all the wild beasts that the Lord God had made," tempts Eve as follows: "You are not going to die [if you eat the fruit "in the middle of the garden"], but God knows that as soon as you eat of it your eyes will be opened and you will be like divine beings who know good and bad."[25]

Adam and Eve both eat the forbidden fruit, then, aware that they are naked, sew together fig leaves and make themselves loincloths. God finds them out, curses the serpent to crawl on his belly, and condemns Eve to the pain of childbirth and the domination of her husband. He condemns Adam to eternal toil. He then makes garments of skins for the pair.

G3:22 – God says, "Now that the man has become like one of us knowing good and bad, what if he should stretch out his hand and take also from the tree of life and eat, and live forever!" God then banishes the man (the text refers only to "the man"), and he

[25]The second part of the passage implies that humanity's real sin was to seek to acquire moral discernment. See also Genesis 3:22.

stations, east of the Garden of Eden, "the cherubim[26] and the fiery ever-turning sword, to guard the way to the tree of life."

Genesis, Chapter 4

Cain and Abel. Cain kills his brother out of jealousy over God's preference for him. God curses Cain, condemns him to become a ceaseless wanderer, and puts a mark on him, so that no one should kill him. God promises "sevenfold vengeance" on anyone who kills Cain.

The rest of the chapter tells about Cain's descendants, as well as the birth of Seth, Adam's second son.

Genesis, Chapter 5

Description of Adam's bloodline, all the way to Noah and the three sons he had when he was 500 years old.

Genesis, Chapter 6

G6:1-4 – Description of "divine beings" (also referred to as "Nephilim") who mate with the daughters of men. The offspring of these unions are "the heroes of old, the men of renown."

Noah and the Ark. G6:5-6 – "The Lord saw how great was man's wickedness on earth and how every plan devised by his mind was nothing but evil all the time. And the Lord regretted that he had been made man on earth, and his heart was saddened." He decides to "put an end to all flesh."

Genesis 6:9-22 – God gives Noah instructions on how to build the Ark, announces that he's going to destroy the world in a flood, and tells Noah to take aboard two of each species. There are two

---

[26] Winged celestial beings.

versions of the instructions: one literary (a pair of each) and one priestly/procedural (extra pairs of clean animals, for sacrifice).

Genesis, Chapter 7
The story of the great flood, which kills all life on earth, except Noah "and those with him in the Ark."

Genesis, Chapter 8
After 150 days, the waters recede, and the Ark comes to rest "on the mountains of Ararat." Three months later, the tops of other mountains become visible. Noah sends out a raven, then a dove, then a dove for the second time. The dove comes back with an olive leaf in its bill. "Then Noah knew that the waters had decreased on the earth." He waits another seven days and sends the dove forth; it doesn't come back. Noah realizes that the earth is dry again.
G8:15ff – God tells Noah to come out of the Ark and bring all the living things with him.
G8:20ff – Noah builds an altar, offers sacrifices to God, who smells the pleasing odor and says to himself: "Never again will I doom the earth because of man, since the devisings of man's mind are evil from his youth; nor will I ever destroy every living being as I have done."

Genesis, Chapter 9
G9:1-3 – God blesses Noah and his sons, tells them to be fertile and increase, and gives them dominion over all living things.
G9:4 – "You must not...eat flesh with its lifeblood in it."
G9:6 – "Whoever sheds the blood of man, By man shall his blood be shed;..."
G9:12-17 – God promises never to destroy the world again and tells

Noah and his sons that "I have set my [rain]bow in the clouds, and it shall serve as a sign of the covenant between me and the earth."
G9:18-28 – Genealogy: how all the world has descended from Noah's three sons, "Ham being the father of Canaan."
The rest of the chapter tells the story of Noah's drunkenness. Noah is inebriated and unclothed in his tent. Ham reports this to his brothers, who place a cloth against their backs and, walking backward so as not to see the shameful sight, cover their father's nakedness. Noah awakes and curses Canaan (i.e., Ham); he declares, "The lowest of slaves to shall he be to his brothers." He blesses the other two brothers.

Noah lives for 350 more years, then dies at the age of 950.

Genesis, Chapter 10
Genealogy of Noah's descendants.

Genesis, Chapter 11
The story of the Tower of Babel.[27] Everyone speaks the same language. They settle in "a valley in the land of Shinar" and decide to build a city and a tower "with its top in the sky, to make a name for ourselves; else we shall be scattered all over the world."
G11:5 – God sees the Tower and says, "If, as one people with one language for all, this is how they have begun to act, then nothing that they may propose to do will be out of their reach."[28] God decides to "confound" their speech, so that they will not be able to understand each other, and he scatters them "from there over the

---

[27] The JPS translation notes (page 19, note *a*) that Babel is another name for Babylon.

[28] God apparently has little use for human aspirations.

face of the whole earth."

The rest of the chapter deals with the genealogy of Shem, whose descendants are Abram, his wife Sarai, and his grandson Lot.

Genesis, Chapter 12

G12:1-7 – God tells Abram to leave his native land and go "to the land that I will show you," because "I will make of you a great nation."

G12:5-9 – Description of Abram's travels. He passes through Canaan and journeys toward the Negeb.

G12:10-13 – There is a famine in the land. Abram goes to Egypt, but before he gets there, he tells his wife that because she is so beautiful, the Egyptians may kill him and take her. He tells her to say that she's his sister "that it may go well with me because of you, and that I may remain alive thanks to you."

G12:14-20 – The Egyptians find Sarai to be beautiful indeed. Pharaoh takes her into her house, and Abraham acquires a great deal of livestock and slaves.

G12:17-20 – But God afflicts Pharaoh and his household "with mighty plagues" because of Sarai. Somehow Pharaoh knows the cause of the trouble. He also knows the truth about the woman he has taken as his wife.[29] He sends for Abram and tells them "Now, here is your wife; take her and be gone!"

Genesis, Chapter 13

Abram and his grandson Lot travel together. Both are very rich – so rich, in fact, "that the land could not support them staying

---

[29] The Torah doesn't explain how he knows all this.

together" and their herdsmen quarrel. Since there is plenty of land, they decide to split up. Lot chooses "the whole plain of the Jordan" and journeys eastward. Abram pitches his tents near Sodom; this is the first we hear of the wickedness of the city's inhabitants.
God promises to Abram all the land he can see, forever.

He also promises to make Abram's offspring as numerous as "the dust of the earth."

Genesis, Chapter 14

G14:1-12 – Long, involved description of wars between obscure tribal chieftains. The kings of Sodom and Gomorrah are on the losing side. Sodom, where Lot had been living, is invaded and pillaged; Lot is captured.

G14:13-15 – Abram gets the news that Lot has been captured. He gathers his 318 retainers,[30] goes in pursuit, defeats the enemy, and brings back Lot and all his people.

G14:17-20 – The king of Sodom greets Abram joyously and blesses God. Abram gives the king one-tenth of his spoils.

G14:21-24 – The king offers Abram all of "the possessions," asking only "the persons" for himself. Abram refuses to take as much as "a thread or a sandal strap of what is yours."

Genesis, Chapter 15

G15:1-6 – God appears to Abram in a dream and tells him that "I am a shield to you; Your reward shall be very great." Abram complains that he has no children, but God assures him that he will – that his offspring will be as numerous as the stars.

---

[30] The JPS translation (p. 24, note a) says that the meaning of the Hebrew word is uncertain.

G15:7-15 – God promises the land to Abram. Abram asks for reassurance. God tells him to bring several animals,[31] which Abram cuts in two (except the young bird).

Abram falls asleep and "a great dark dread descended upon him." God tells him, "Know well that your offspring shall be strangers in a land not theirs, and they shall be enslaved and oppressed 400 years; but I will execute judgment on the nation they shall serve, and in the end they shall go free with great wealth." Abram is to live to a ripe old age.

G15:17-21 – "When the sun set and it was very dark, there appeared a smoking oven, and a flaming torch which passed between those pieces."[32] On that day, God makes the land-promise, the covenant with Abram. The rest of the chapter enumerates the tribes whose land God will give to Abram's offspring.

<u>Genesis, Chapter 16</u>

G16:1-6 – Since Sarai, Abram's wife, has borne him no children, she asks her husband to have sex with Hagar, an Egyptian maid-servant. Hagar gets pregnant, and now Sarai becomes very upset, thinking her maid no longer respects her. Abram tells her to do whatever she wants; she treats Hagar harshly, and Hagar runs away.

G16:7-16 – An angel finds Hagar by a spring and sends her back to her mistress with the promise of numerous offspring. Hagar bears a son to Abram, now 86. They call him Ishmael.

---

[31] And he is very particular: "a three-year-old she-goat, a three-year-old ram..."

[32] Hillman (p. 66) says that Abram is still dreaming all of this.

Genesis, Chapter 17

G17:1-14 – God appears before Abram, now 99, and tells him that he will be "the father of a multitude of nations" and that his name is now Abraham. Once again God promises land to Abraham's offspring, forever. Part of the bargain is circumcision at the age of eight days. This includes slaves. "Thus shall my covenant be marked in your flesh as an everlasting pact."

G17:15-22 – God tells Abraham's wife that her name is now Sarah ("princess") and promises that she "shall give rise to nations; rulers of peoples shall issue from her." God tells Sarah that she will bear a son named Isaac who will be "the father of twelve chieftains, and I will make of him a great nation."

G17:23-27 – Abraham circumcises Ishmael and everyone in his household, including his slaves.

Genesis, Chapter 18

G18:1-8 – Abraham sees three men standing near him as he sits at the entrance of his tents. He bows down to them and offers refreshments. Abraham tells Sarah to make cakes. He prepares a calf for the strangers and gives them curds and milk.[33]

G18:9-15 – One of the strangers says that Abraham and Sarah will have a son. Sarah, who had stopped having periods, laughs to herself. God asks Abraham why Sarah laughed. Sarah is frightened[34] and says that she didn't laugh. But God says, "You did laugh."

G18:16-21 – The strangers leave. God is thinking to himself (the text

---

[33] This was before the dietary laws went into effect.

[34] The Torah doesn't say why she's frightened, but presumably she figures that God is not going to take kindly to her doubt of him.

reports this as actual speech on God's part). He wonders whether he should tell Abraham, with whom he has made a covenant and whom he has promised such greatness, about what he's going to do. He says he's going to go to Sodom and Gomorrah "to see whether they have acted...according to the outcry that has reached me."
G18:22-32 – Abraham bargains with God about the destruction of Sodom and Gomorrah: "Will you sweep away the innocent along with the guilty?... Far be it from you to do such a thing, to bring death upon the innocent as well as the guilty." He gets God to concede that if there are as few as ten innocent people in the city, he won't destroy it.

<u>Genesis, Chapter 19</u>

The destruction of Sodom and Gomorrah. 19:1-3 – Two angels arrive in Sodom. Lot is sitting at the gate of the city when they arrive. He invites them to his house and prepares a feast for them.
G19:4-9 – All the townspeople (the men, that is) "young and old." come to Lot's house and shout to Lot that they want the visitors to come out "that we may be intimate with them." Lot begs them to desist and offers his two virgin daughters instead.
G19:9-11 – The Sodomites threaten Lot. The visitors pull him into the house and shut the door. The people outside are "struck with blinding light, so that they were helpless to find the entrance."
G19:12-14 – The visitors urge Lot to get his whole family out of the city because God is going to destroy it.
G19:15-22 – Despite Lot's reluctance, the angels take him by the hand and lead him out of the city. They tell him to flee to the hills. Lot is concerned that he won't survive if he flees that far, so he asks that his life be saved if he flees to a small town called Zoar. God agrees not to destroy Sodom until Lot gets to Zoar.

G19:23-26 – God annihilates Sodom and Gomorrah with "sulfurous fire" from heaven. Lot's wife looks back and is turned into a pillar of salt.
G19:30-38 – Lot and his two daughters leave Zoar and live in a cave. His daughters, believing that there are no men left in the world, get him drunk and commit incest with him in order to "maintain life through our father." They bear two sons, who become the fathers of the Moabites and Ammonites.

Genesis, Chapter 20
G20:1-7 – Abraham continues his travels. Again he tells people that Sarah is his sister. The local king, Abimelech, sends for her, but God comes to him in a dream and tells them he's going to die if he takes Sarah, because she is a married woman. The king protests his innocence. God agrees with him and tells him to "restore the man's wife."
G20:8-13 – The king summons Abraham and demands to know the reason for the deception. Abraham says that he was afraid that they would kill him. "And besides, she is in truth my sister, my father's daughter though not my mother's; and she became my wife."
G20:14-18 – All's well that ends well: the king restores Sarah to Abraham, gives him livestock and slaves, and tells him he can settle wherever he wants. God then heals the king, as well as his wife and slave girls, so that they can bear children – he had previously "closed fast every womb of the household of Abimelech" because of Sarah.

Genesis, Chapter 21

G21:1-8 – When Abraham is 100 years old, Sarah bears him a son, Isaac.

G21:9-13 – Sarah tells Abraham to cast out Hagar and her son. Abraham is distressed, but God tells him to do as Sarah says, because his line will be continued through Isaac, and as for the other son, "I will make a nation of him, too."

G21:14-20 – Abraham gives Hagar and her son some bread and water and sends them away. Hagar wanders about in the wilderness of Beersheba and is ready to leave her son to die, but an angel calls to her from heaven and tells her to "lift up the boy and hold him by the hand, for I will make a great nation of him."

G21:22-34 – King Abimelech and Phicol, the "chief of his troops," initiate a loyalty pact with Abraham, because "God is with you in everything that you do." Abraham gives the king sheep and oxen. He also gives the king seven ewes, as a good-faith gesture and proof that he had in fact dug a well that the king's servants had seized earlier. The pact is concluded, "and Abraham resided in the land of the Philistines a long time."

Genesis, Chapter 22

The binding of Isaac. G22:1-14 – "Sometime afterward, God put Abraham to the test." He tells Abraham that he must offer his son Isaac as a burnt offering. Abraham obeys and begins preparations. He binds Isaac and is ready to kill his son, when an angel appears and tells him that he has passed the test. Abraham looks up, sees a ram, and offers it in place of his son.

G22:15-19 – The angel calls to Abraham again and tells him that God has said that as a result of this show of loyalty, I will "make your descendants as numerous as the stars of heaven and the sands on the seashore; and your descendants shall seize the gates of their foes. All the nations of the earth shall bless themselves by your descendants, because you have obeyed my command."

Genesis, Chapter 23

G23:1-9 – Sarah dies at the age of 127. Since Abraham is a resident alien among the Hittites, he asks them to sell him a burial site. They agree, offering him the choicest of places. Abraham asks them to intercede with a Hittite named Ephron and get him to sell Abraham a cave at the edge of his land.

G23:10-20 – Ephron offers to give Abraham the field and cave, but eventually they agree on 400 shekels of silver "at the going merchants' rate." Abraham buries Sarah in the cave.

Genesis, Chapter 24

G24:1-9 – Abraham, who is now "old, advanced in years," asks his senior household servant to "put your hand under my thigh"[35] and swear to go to the land of Abraham's birth and get a wife for Isaac. The servant asks what to do if the woman doesn't consent to come back with him. Abraham says that whatever happens, his servant must not take Isaac back there, since God had told him that "I will assign this land [i.e., where Abraham is now] to your offspring." He tells the servant that God will send an angel before him, to help him get a wife for Isaac.

G24:10-14 – The servant takes ten camels and "all the bounty of his master" and goes to the city of Nahor. He makes his camels kneel down by the well outside the city in the evening, when the women come to draw water. He asks God to give him a sign: whichever maiden agrees to water his camels will be the one for Isaac.

[35] I.e., swear on his testicles.

G24:15-20 – The beautiful virgin Rebekah (who, the text notes, is actually the granddaughter of Abraham's brother Nahor) agrees to give water to the servant and his camels.
G24:21-27 – The servant produces some gold – a ring and two armbands – and asks if there's room in her father's house to spend the night. She says that there is.
G24:28-33 – Rebekah's brother Laban invites the servant and the camels to his house. But the man won't eat "until I have told my tale."
G24:34-49 – The servant recounts the entire story of how he was sent out by Abraham and came to find Rebekah.
G24:50-61 – Rebekah's father and brother agree to the match. The servant gives everyone gifts. Everyone eats and drinks. The next morning, Rebekah and her nurse set out with Abraham's servant and his men.
G24:62-67 – Isaac is walking in the field toward evening, looks up, and sees everyone coming back. Upon hearing that the man they are looking at is Isaac, Rebekah covers herself with her veil. The servant tells Isaac the whole story, and Isaac brings Rebecca "into the tent of his mother Sarah, and he took Rebekah as his wife."

Genesis, Chapter 25

G25:1-18 – Abraham takes another wife; the text describes their lineage. Abraham dies at the "good ripe age" of 175 and is buried by his sons Isaac and Ishmael. The text describes Ishmael's descendants.
G25:19-23 – Isaac pleads with God on behalf of his wife, because "she was barren." With God's help, she conceives. She feels the babies struggling in her womb. God tells her that it's because "two nations are in your womb, two separate peoples shall issue from your body; the one people shall be mightier than the other, and the

older shall serve the younger."
G25:24-34 – **Jacob and Esau.** The latter is the first to be born; he "emerged red," with a "hairy mantle all over." His name is a play on the Hebrew word for "hair." Jacob is born second, holding on to his brother's heel. His name is a play on the Hebrew word for "heel."[36] The boys grow up. Esau becomes a skillful hunter, a "man of the outdoors; but Jacob was a mild man who stayed in camp." One day, a starving Esau comes upon his brother, who persuades him to sell his birthright for food.

Genesis, Chapter 26

G26:1-5 – There is a famine in the land, but God tells Isaac to "stay in the land which I point out to you." God promises the land to Isaac and his heirs.
G26:6-11 – Like father, like son: Isaac tells everyone that Rebekah is his sister, fearing, like Abraham, that he'll be killed for this beautiful woman. Eventually the same king – Abimelech – finds out the truth when he sees Isaac fondling his wife. The king decrees that anyone who molests either of them will be put to death.
G26:12-16 – Isaac becomes very rich. The Philistines envy him and plug up the wells that Abraham's servants had dug. The king tells Isaac to go away "for you have become far too big for us."
G26:17-22 – Isaac leaves, digs new wells, contends with the herdsmen of the region over the wells, and finally digs a well that is not disputed by anyone.
G26:23-30 – God appears to Isaac and promises that "I will bless

---

[36] JPS translation, page 45, notes *c* and *d*. There are many examples of this custom of naming children for the circumstances of their birth. Places are often named for the events that occurred there.

you and increase your offspring for the sake of my servant Abraham." Isaac builds an altar. The king and his senior officials, having witnessed God's appearance, offer a sworn treaty. Everybody has a feast.
G26:31-35 – Isaac departs after exchanging oaths with the king and his people. A new well is dug. At the age of 40, Esau takes two wives, "and they were a source of bitterness to Isaac and Rebekah."

Genesis, Chapter 27
The betrayal of Esau by Jacob. Isaac, old and nearly blind, tells Esau to bring him some meat and he, Isaac, will bestow his blessing before he dies. But Rebekah overhears and tells Jacob to bring two choice kids, and she'll prepare them instead – and cover Jacob's hands with their skins, so that Isaac will think he's touching Esau. The ruse works: Isaac bestows his blessing on Jacob.
Esau returns, and the awful truth is discovered. Jacob has taken his birthright and now his blessing too. He begs his father to bless him as well, so Isaac says that "your abode shall enjoy the fat of the earth...yet by your sword you shall live, and you shall serve your brother; but when you grow restive, you shall break his yoke from your neck."
G27:41-45 – Esau bears a grudge against his brother and vows to kill him after the mourning period of his father's death. Rebekah tells him to run away and stay with her brother Laban until Esau's anger subsides.

Genesis, Chapter 28
G28:1-5 – Isaac blesses Jacob, tells him not to take a Canaanite wife, and sends him off.
G28:6-9 – Esau, realizing his father's disapproval of Canaanite women, takes another wife – the daughter of Ishmael.

G28:10-22 – **Jacob and the ladder.** Jacob stops for the night and lies down to sleep. He dreams of a stairway[37] reaching from the ground to the sky, "and angels of God were going up and down on it." God appears to Jacob in a dream and promises to him and his offspring the ground on which he is lying. Jacob awakens, deeply moved by the dream. He's sure he has experienced God's presence. He promises that if God protects him on his journey and returns him safely to his father's house, then he'll always be loyal to God and set aside a tithe for him.

Genesis, Chapter 29

G29:1-14 – Jacob comes into "the land of the Easterners." At a well, he meets his cousin Rachel and tells her who he is. Rachel fetches her uncle Laban, who is overjoyed to see Jacob.

G29:15-20 – Laban asks Jacob what his wages will be, and Jacob replies that he'll work for seven years if he can have the beautiful Rachel – "and they seemed to him but a few days because of his love for her."

G29:21-30 – Jacob tells Laban that it's time for him to have Rachel. But Laban deceives Jacob and brings him Leah instead. Jacob cohabits with her before he discovers the truth. He is (understandably) upset, but Laban says that "It is not the practice in our place to marry off the younger before the older." He tells Jacob to wait for the end of the bridal week and he'll give him Leah too, provided he serves another seven years. Jacob agrees.

G29:31-35 – Leah bears three sons: Judah, Reuben, and Levi.

Genesis, Chapter 30

---

[37] Other translations are "ramp" or "ladder." JPS, p. 51, note *b*.

G30:1-8 – Rachel wants to have children too, but cannot. She gives her maid Bilhah to Jacob. Bilhah bears two sons. Leah gives her own maid to Jacob as concubine; two sons result.
G30:14-24 – Rachel promises Leah that Jacob will lie with her (Leah) in return for some mandrakes[38] that Reuben finds in the field. Rachel tells her husband, in effect, "You have to sleep with Leah – I paid mandrakes for you. " Leah bears two sons and a daughter, Dinah. God enables Rachel to bear a son, whom she names Joseph.[39]
G30:25-36 – Jacob tells his uncle that he's ready to go back home. Laban asks, "What should I pay you?" Jacob says he'll "again pasture and keep your flocks" if Laban will let him go through the whole flock and take "every dark-colored sheep and every spotted and speckled goat" for his wages. But later that same day, Laban removes all the aforementioned sheep and goats and leaves them in charge of his son. "He put a distance of three days' journey between himself and Jacob, while Jacob was pasturing the rest of Laban's flock."
G30:37-43 – Jacob outwits Laban by breeding his own flock of streaked and spotted goats and dark colored sheep. He also mates the sturdier animals with each other. He thus grows "exceedingly prosperous" and comes to "own large flocks, maidservants and manservants, camels and asses."

---

[38] A Eurasian plant that has purple flowers and a branched root thought to resemble the human body; widely believed to have magical powers.

[39] The text notes that Joseph's name resembles the Hebrew words for "take away" and "add", as in, respectively, "God has taken away my disgrace" and "May the Lord add another son for me."

Genesis, Chapter 31

G31:1-13 – Laban's sons are grumbling about Jacob's good fortune, but Jacob says that it's all God's doing. He reports a dream in which "the he-goats mating with the flock are streaked, speckled, and mottled"; an angel tells him that God is taking care of him and that he should return to his native land.

G31:14-16 – Rachel and Leah wonder whether they still have a share of their inheritance. They think their father Laban regards them as "outsiders, now that he has sold us and has used up our purchase price." They conclude that "all the wealth that God has taken away from our father belongs to us and to our children."

G31:17-18 – Jacob puts his children and wives on camels and drives out all his livestock and wealth.

G31:19 – While Laban is shearing his sheep, Rachel steals his household idols.

G31:20 – Jacob never told Laban that he was fleeing.

G31:22-24 – "On the third day, Laban was told that Jacob had fled." He catches up with him. God appears to Laban in a dream and warns him against attempting anything "good or bad" in regard to Jacob.

G31:25-35 – Laban confronts Jacob and berates him for fleeing secretly. "I would have sent you off with festive music, with timbral and lyre." Then Laban recalls God's warning and says,"Very well, you had to leave because you were longing for your father's house; but why did you steal my gods?" Jacob explains that he fled because he thought Laban might "take your daughters from me by force." But he doesn't know anything about the stolen gods. Laban searches everywhere but can't find them because Rachel has hidden them under a cushion.

G31:36-44 – Now it's Jacob's turn to become aggrieved. He resents

the implication of theft. He recounts the difficulties of his labor under Laban. Laban admits that his ownership of his daughters is now dubious and suggests a pact.
G31:45-54 – Laban and Jacob arrange stones into a mound, eat a meal, and mark out their respective territories. Also, Laban says that if Jacob doesn't treat Rachel and Leah well, God will know about it.

Genesis, Chapter 32
G32:1-8 – Jacob and Laban part ways. Jacob sends a messenger ahead to Esau to tell them that his brother is returning with many gifts. The messengers come back and tell Jacob that Esau is coming with 400 men. Jacob is frightened and divides his people into two camps, thinking that one might survive an attack.
G32:10-13 – Jacob prays to God to deliver him from Esau's vengeance.
G32:14-22 – Jacob divides into droves the various livestock he's going to give to Esau. He sends them ahead, one drove at a time, to "propitiate him with presents in advance."
G32:23-33 – **Jacob's wrestling match.** After sending all his family and possessions across the stream, "Jacob was left alone. And a man wrestled with him until the break of dawn." Jacob's hip is strained. He refuses to let go unless the other wrestler blesses him. The man replies that Jacob's name will now be Israel (derived from the Hebrew word for "strive") because he has "striven with beings divine and human and [has] prevailed." Jacob names the place Peniel, i.e., "I have seen a divine being face-to-face, yet my life has been preserved." G32:33 – "That is why the children of Israel to this day do not eat the thigh muscle that is on the socket of the hip..."

Genesis, Chapter 33

Jacob sees Esau coming with 400 men. He divides the children among Leah, Rachel, and the maids and goes on ahead to meet Esau, bowing low to the ground. But the brothers reconcile happily and plan to go back together. Jacob tells Esau to go ahead because traveling too fast would be harmful to his flocks. Esau agrees, and Jacob goes to a place called Succoth, so called because that's where he built stalls (*succoth*) for his cattle.

Genesis, Chapter 34

Dinah, the daughter of Jacob and Leah, is raped by Schechem, the son of the local chieftain, Hamor the Hivite. Jacob's sons are understandably angry, but Hamor asks for Dinah in marriage and invites Jacob and his relatives to settle in the Hivites' land. Jacob's sons agree – but only if all the men of the other tribe are circumcised.

On the third day, when all the Hivites are still in pain from the circumcision, Simeon and Levi, two of Jacob's sons, go into the city and kill all the men. The other sons of Jacob plunder the town and seize all of its wealth. They take the wives and children as captives.

Jacob scolds his sons, because their actions will cause trouble with other local tribes. But they answer, "Should our sister be treated like a whore?"

Genesis, Chapter 35

G35:1-4 – God tells Jacob to go to Bethel and build an altar. Jacob and his household bury their idols and set out.

G35:5 – "... a terror from God fell on the cities roundabout, so that they did not pursue the sons of Jacob."

G35:9-15 – God tells Jacob his name shall henceforth be "Israel," promises to Jacob the land he had assigned to Abraham and Isaac, and tells Jacob that "Kings shall issue from your loins."
G35:16-26 – Rachel has another son, Benjamin, but dies in childbirth. Jacob, with his wives and concubines, now has 12 sons.
G35:27-29 – Isaac dies at the age of 180.

Genesis, Chapter 36
Genealogy of Esau and his descendants.

Genesis, Chapter 37
Joseph and his brothers. G37:1-4 – Joseph is 17 and is tending the flocks with his brothers, helping two of his father's wives. "And Joseph brought bad reports of them to their father." Jacob loves Joseph best, because he's the child of old age; he makes him "an ornamented tunic."[40] Joseph's brothers hate and envy him even more.
G37:5-8 – Joseph tells his brothers about his dream: they're binding sheaves in the field, when suddenly his sheaf stands up and remains upright, and the others bow low to it. The brothers get the obvious symbolism and hate him even more.
G37:9-11 – Joseph has another dream: the sun, the moon, and 11 stars are bowing down to him. The brothers hate him even more.
G37:12-24 – Jacob[41] sends Joseph out to where his brothers are pasturing. They see him coming and plan to kill him, but Reuben

[40] Or "a coat of many colors"; the meaning of the Hebrew is uncertain (JPS, p. 70, note *a*).

[41] The JPS translation uses both *Jacob* and *Israel*. For consistency and ease of understanding, I'll stick with *Jacob*.

convinces them to shed no blood and to throw him into a pit (planning to save him later). Before they do, they strip him of his ornamented tunic.
G37:25-28 – The brothers decide not to kill Joseph but to sell him to Midianite traders for 20 pieces of silver.
G37:29-36 – Reuben comes back but finds Joseph gone. The brothers have dipped the ornamental tunic in goat's blood. They take it to Jacob, who is devastated by the thought of his son's death. The Midianites sell Joseph in Egypt, to the chief steward of the Pharaoh.

<u>Genesis, Chapter 38</u>
The story of Judah, one of Jacob's sons.
G38:1-11 – Judah has three sons – Shelah, Er and Onan. Er is displeasing to the Lord, who takes his life. Judah tells Onan to join with his brother's wife, but Onan, knowing the seed would not count as his, spills it on the ground. This also displeases God, who kills Onan. Judah tells Er's wife Tamar to live with him until Shelah grows up.
G38:12-19 – Much time passes, and Judah's wife dies. Judah heads for Timnah for the sheepshearing. Tamar is told that her father-in-law is coming and meets him on the road, because Shelah is grown up, but she hasn't been given to him as wife. She covers her face with a veil, and Judah takes her for a prostitute. He promises to pay her with a kid from his flock. She asks, as a pledge, for his "seal and cord, and the staff which you carry." Judah agrees and unwittingly has sex with his daughter-in-law.
G39:20-23 – Judah sends the kid with a friend, but the man can't find Tamar. He asks people where the cult prostitute is, and they don't know of any such person.

G39:24-30 – Three months later, Judah is told that his daughter-in-law is "with child by harlotry." He orders her brought out to be burned, but she sends a message to him that "I am with child by the man to whom these belong" - referring, of course, to the seal, cord and staff. Judah recognizes them and admits that "she is more in the right than I, inasmuch as I did not give her to my son Shelah." Tamar gives birth to twins.

Genesis, Chapter 39

Joseph is doing very well in Egypt. The Pharaoh's steward takes a liking to him and puts him in charge of the entire household. Since Joseph was well built and handsome, the steward's wife keeps trying to seduce him, but he refuses. One day she grabs his garment and he flees. She tells the servants, and eventually the steward himself, that Joseph had come "to me to dally with me," but when she screamed, he fled. The steward is furious and throws Joseph into prison, but because God was with him, he does well even there: the chief jailer puts him in charge of all the prisoners.

Genesis, Chapter 40

Pharaoh, displeased with his cup bearer and baker, throws them both into jail, where they meet Joseph. Some time later, both have dreams, which they ask Joseph to interpret. Joseph tells the cup bearer that his dream means that Pharaoh will pardon him. Joseph asks the cup bearer to "think of me when all is well with you again, and do me the kindness of mentioning me to Pharaoh, so as to free me from this place." The baker's dream means that his head will be impaled upon a pole. Both interpretations turn out to be correct, but the cup bearer forgets all about Joseph.

Genesis, Chapter 41

G41:1-24 – Pharaoh has two dreams - one of seven ugly, gaunt cows who devour seven handsome and sturdy cows, another about seven thin and scorched ears of grain which devour seven solid and full ears. None of the magicians of Egypt can interpret the dreams, but the cup bearer remembers about Joseph and his accuracy at dream interpretation. Joseph is rushed from the dungeon and gets a haircut and a change of clothing before he appears before Pharaoh.
G41:25-35 – Joseph explains that Pharaoh's dreams are revelations from God about what he is about to do: seven years of abundance will be followed by seven years of famine. Joseph recommends that Pharaoh "find a man of discernment and wisdom and set him over the land of Egypt" to supervise the storing of grain during the good years.
G41:37-57 – Pharaoh thinks that it's a great idea and puts Joseph in charge as his second-in-command. As predicted, seven years of plenty ensue, and Joseph collects the abundance. Then comes the famine, and Joseph rations out grain to the Egyptians – in fact, to the whole world, "for the famine had become severe throughout the world."

Genesis, Chapter 42
G42:1-5 – Jacob sends ten of his sons to Egypt to get food; he doesn't send Benjamin, "since he feared that he might meet with disaster."
G42:6-17 – Joseph pretends not to recognize his brothers; they don't recognize him. He accuses them of being spies, which they deny. Joseph tells them he will put them to the test by detaining all but one, who will go back and bring his youngest brother.
G42:18-28 – On the third day, Joseph tells them that he's only going

to hold one of them, while the rest bring food back to their households. But they still have to bring him their youngest brother. The brothers tell one another they're being punished because of what they did to Joseph, and Reuben says, "Did I not tell you, 'Do no wrong to the boy'?...Now comes the reckoning for his blood." (The text notes that they speak to Joseph through an interpreter, so they don't know that Joseph understands what they're saying.)

Joseph keeps Simeon and allows the rest to go, their bags filled with grain – and their money. On the way back, one of them discovers the money, and they all become frightened.

G42:29-34 – The brothers return to Jacob and tell him what has happened.

G42:35-38 – The brothers all discover that Joseph has returned their money. Everyone is dismayed. Reuben volunteers to go to Egypt and bring back Simeon. He tells Jacob that Jacob can kill his - Reuben's - two sons if he doesn't bring Simeon back. But Jacob won't let him go.

Genesis, Chapter 43

G43:1-10 – The famine continues, and Joseph's family finishes all the food they had brought from Egypt. Joseph tells them to go get more. But Judah reminds his father that they have to bring their brother. He says he'll take responsibility for the boy, because if they don't go, they'll starve.

G43:11-14 – Jacob finally agrees and sends the brothers to Egypt with twice the money - and gifts as well.

G43:15-28 – The brothers make their way to Egypt and present themselves to Joseph. He invites them into his house to dine. But they're afraid that he's going to seize them and enslave them, because of the money that had been replaced in their bags. They tell Joseph's steward about the money, and he reassures them – and brings out Simeon.

Joseph returns, and the brothers bow low. He asks about their father. He sees Benjamin and, on the verge of tears, goes into a room and weeps. He regains his composure, comes back and orders the meal to be served.

Joseph, the brothers, and the other Egyptians are all served separately, because "the Egyptians could not dine with the Hebrews, since that would be abhorrent to the Egyptians."

Genesis, Chapter 44

G44:1-5 – Joseph tells his steward to load the men's bags with food, to give them their money back - and to put his silver goblet in the youngest brother's bag. Then, just after the brothers leave the city, Joseph sends his steward after them to accuse them of stealing the goblet.

G44:6-13 – The brothers deny stealing anything and tell the steward that if the accusation is true, whoever stole the goblet shall die and the rest of them will become slaves. The steward says that only the one who has the goblet will be a slave. The goblet turns up in Benjamin's bag, the brothers rend their clothes, reload their animals, and return to the city.

G44:14-17 – The brothers go back to Joseph's house and throw themselves on the ground before him. They protest their innocence. Joseph tells them that only the one who actually had the goblet will be a slave; the rest of them can return in peace.

G44:18-34 – Judah tells Joseph everything that went on between the brothers and Jacob on their previous trip home. He says that if Benjamin doesn't come back, Jacob will die. He offers himself as a slave instead.

Genesis, Chapter 45

Joseph can no longer control himself. He has all his attendants withdraw and begins crying out loud. He tells his brothers the truth and urges them not to "be distressed or reproach yourselves because you sold me hither; it was to save life that God sent me ahead of you...to ensure your survival on earth, and to save your lives in an extraordinary deliverance."

He tells the brothers that they can dwell in the region of Goshen and that he'll provide for them, since there will be five more years of famine. He kisses his brothers; everyone weeps for joy.

The news reaches Pharaoh's palace, and Pharaoh orders that Jacob and his households come to Egypt, where they can "live off the fat of the land." Joseph loads his brothers up with provisions and gifts for his father and sends them on their way.

The brothers arrive in Canaan and give Jacob the good news. Jacob's spirit is revived, and he says he'll go to Egypt and see Joseph.

<u>Genesis, Chapter 46</u>

Jacob sets out for Egypt. God calls to him in a vision and reassures him that the divine presence will be with him.

G46:5-27 – Enumeration of all of the Israelites who came to Egypt (Jacob's household totals 70).

G46:28-34 – Joseph goes to Goshen to meet his father. He tells his brothers that if they tell Pharaoh they are shepherds, they will be allowed to remain in Goshen, "for all shepherds are abhorrent to Egyptians."

<u>Genesis, Chapter 47</u>

G47:1-11 – Joseph tells Pharaoh that his family has come from Canaan. He introduces Jacob to Pharaoh, who gives Joseph's father

and brothers "holdings in the choicest part of the land of Egypt."
G47:13-27 – The famine continues. The Egyptians and the Canaanites give Joseph all their money in exchange for rations. After a year, when the people have no more money, Joseph provides food in exchange for their livestock. The next year, they have nothing left to give Joseph but their land in exchange for food, so "Joseph gained possession of all the farmland of Egypt for Pharaoh." Joseph then gives the people seed, in exchange for the promise that one-fifth of their harvest will go to Pharaoh (except for the land of the priests).
G47:28-31 – Seventeen years pass; Jacob is now 147 years old. He makes Joseph promise to bury him with his fathers.

Genesis, Chapter 48

Jacob is ill. Joseph brings his two sons, Manasseh and Ephraim, to their grandfather's bedside. Jacob tells Joseph that God had appeared to him in a vision promising to make him "fertile and numerous" and giving his offspring the land of Canaan forever.

Then Jacob tells Joseph that the latter's two sons "shall be mine no less than Reuben and Simeon." Jacob blesses Joseph's two sons and Joseph as well.

He tells Joseph, "I am about to die; but God will be with you and bring you back to the land of your fathers."

Genesis, Chapter 49

Jacob calls all of his sons together "that I may tell you what is to befall you in days to come." He then articulates poetic prophecies about each of the twelve tribes. After giving instructions about where he is to be buried, Jacob dies.

Genesis, Chapter 50

G50:1-14 – The grief-stricken Joseph weeps, kisses his father, and orders the physicians to embalm him. After a mourning period of 70 days, Joseph asks Pharaoh's permission to bury Jacob in Canaan.

Pharaoh agrees, so Joseph, all of Pharaoh's officials, Joseph's household and everybody but the children go to the burial site, where they observe a mourning period of seven days.

G50:15-21 – Joseph's brothers are still worried that he might bear a grudge against them. They send a message to Joseph, to the effect that Jacob wanted him to forgive his brothers. Joseph tells them not to worry about it because "although you intended me harm, God intended it for good, so as to bring about the present result – the survival of many people."

G50:22-26 – Joseph dies at the age of 110.

EXODUS

Exodus, Chapter 1

E1:1-7 – Joseph, his brothers, and their whole generation are all dead. "But the Israelites were fertile and prolific; they multiplied and increased very greatly, so that the land was filled with them."

E1:8-14 – Egypt has a new Pharaoh, and this one "did not know Joseph." He is not happy about how numerous the Israelites have become; he fears that they may join with Egypt's enemies. Oppression begins. But the more the Israelites are oppressed, "the more they increase and spread out."

E1:15-22 – Pharaoh tells the Hebrew midwives to kill all the male Jewish babies. The midwives, fearing God, disobey. When Pharaoh asks them why they have let the boys live, they tell him that Jewish women are so vigorous that they give birth before the midwife can come to them. God rewards the midwives. Pharaoh tells the Egyptians to kill all the male Jewish babies.

Exodus, Chapter 2

E2:1-10 – **Moses' childhood.** A man and a woman from the tribe of Levi give birth to a boy. His mother, seeing how beautiful he is, hides him for three months. Finally, when she can hide him no longer, she puts him in a caulked wicker basket "among the reeds by the bank of the Nile....his sister stationed herself in the distance, to learn what would befall him."

The baby is discovered by Pharaoh's daughter, who knows he's a Hebrew child. Moses' sister asks if she should get a Hebrew nurse, and the Pharaoh's daughter agrees. So Moses is returned to his real mother until he grows up, when he is brought to Pharaoh's daughter and made her son. That's when he's named Moses, which means "I drew him out of the water."[42]

E2:11-15 – **Moses' murder of the Egyptian.** Moses is now a young man. He sees an Egyptian beating one of his Hebrew kinsman and kills the Egyptian. The next day, he sees two Hebrews fighting and tries to stop them. One of them answers, "Who made you chief and ruler over us? Do you mean to kill me as you killed the Egyptian?" Moses is frightened; he assumes, correctly, that Pharaoh knows about the incident. Moses flees to the land of Midian and sits down beside a well.

E2:16-21 – Seven daughters of the priests of Midian come to water their flocks, but shepherds drive them away. Moses defends them. They go back and tell their father what has happened, and he

[42] The name is related to the Hebrew word for "to draw out" (JPS, p. 104, note *a*).

invites Moses to break bread with him. Moses agrees to stay with him and to accept one of his daughters, Zipporah, as his wife.
E2:23-25 – Much time passes. Pharaoh dies. The Israelites' groans and cries are heard by God, who remembers his covenant with the three patriarchs.

Exodus, Chapter 3

The burning bush. Moses is at Mount Horeb tending the flock of his father-in-law Jethro when an angel appears in a burning bush (which does not burn up). God calls to Moses and tells him to remove his sandals, because he is on holy ground. God tells Moses who he is, and Moses hides his face in fear.
E3:7-10 – God tells Moses that he is aware of the Israelites' suffering and has come down to rescue them and bring them to a land of milk and honey; he enumerates the tribes whose lands he's promising. He tells Moses that "you shall free my people...". Moses is dubious, but God says that he'll be with him all the way. Moses asks God's name, and God tells him.[43]
E3:16-22 – God tells Moses to assemble the elders of Israel and tell them that God has appeared to him and promised to take them out of Egypt and give them the land of the Canaanites and other tribes.

---

[43] The various Hebrew names of God and their various meanings are the source of much philosophical and theological speculation, which is not the purpose of this book. I am, of course, concerned with the basic linguistic facts: (1) the meaning of the Hebrew is highly uncertain, as evidenced by the various translations – 'I am that I am'; 'I will be what I will be'; etc. (the alternatives and the *etc.* are from JPS, p. 106, note *a*); and (2) the name, as it appears in the Torah, is written with the Hebrew equivalents of YHWH (whence "Yahweh" and "Jehovah"). A superstitious fear prevents traditional Jews from pronouncing this word phonetically; instead, it is pronounced "adonai," which means 'the Lord' or sometimes "hashem," 'the name.'

He further tells Moses that he and the elders should go three days into the wilderness and make a sacrifice to God. God promises that he will smite the Egyptians and allow the Israelites to strip them of their possessions.

Exodus, Chapter 4

E4:1-9 – Moses is concerned that the Israelites won't believe him, so God tells him to cast his rod on the ground, whereupon it turns into a snake, then back to a rod. God tells Moses to put his hand into his bosom, and when he takes it out it's encrusted with snowy scales; he puts it back and takes it out again, and it's good as new. God says that if they don't believe these signs, Moses is to take some water from the Nile and pour it on the ground, and it will turn into blood.

E4:10-19 – Moses protests that he is not a man of words. God replies, "Who gives man speech?... is it not I, the Lord? Now go...". But Moses is still reluctant. God gets angry. He tells Moses that Moses' brother Aaron will be his spokesman, "with you playing the role of God to him." Moses takes leave of Jethro and, with the Lord's assurance that all the men who sought to kill him are now dead, sets out for Egypt.

E4:21-23 – God tells Moses that he is to "perform before Pharaoh all the marvels that I have put within your power." God also says that he'll stiffen Pharaoh's heart so that "he will not let the people go."

E4:24-26 – "At a night encampment on the way, the Lord encountered him[44] and sought to kill him." Zipporah circumcises

[44] Hillman (p. 158) calls this "one of the Torah's most enigmatic passages," and with good reason. Apparently God, for reasons of his own, had decided to kill Moses, but Zipporah's quick thinking saves him.

her son, and God "let[s] him alone."
E4:27-31 – God tells Aaron to go meet his brother. Moses tells Aaron about God's commitment and the "signs," i.e., the magic that God had instructed him to perform. They gather all the elders, give them God's message, perform the signs, and the people are convinced: "they bowed low in homage."

<u>Exodus, Chapter 5</u>

Moses and Aaron go to Pharaoh and tell him that God has said "Let my people go" so that they can celebrate a festival for him in the wilderness. Pharaoh is annoyed that Moses and Aaron want to distract the people from their labors. To make them work harder, he decrees that the taskmasters shall no longer provide straw to make bricks; the Israelites now have to make the same quota of bricks, but they have to gather the straw themselves.

The foremen of the Israelites are angry with Moses and Aaron for making their burden even heavier. Moses complains to God: "Ever since I came to Pharaoh to speak in your name, he has dealt worse with this people; and still you have not delivered your people."

<u>Exodus, Chapter 6</u>

E6:1-9 – God tells Moses to tell the Israelites that he, God, will free them "with outstretched arm and through extraordinary chastisements" and will bring them into the land which he swore to give to Abraham, Isaac, and Jacob. But the Israelites don't listen to Moses, "their spirits crushed by cruel bondage." God sends Moses and Aaron to talk to Pharaoh again.
E6:14-25 – Genealogy of the various Israelite clans.

<u>Exodus, Chapter 7</u>

E7:1-7 – Once again God promises extraordinary punishments upon the Egyptians. Also: "I will harden Pharaoh's heart, that I may multiply my signs and marvels in the land of Egypt."[45]
E7:8-13 – Moses and Aaron appear before Pharaoh. Aaron turns his rod into a serpent. But Pharaoh summons his wise men and sorcerers, and the Egyptian magicians turn their rods into serpents too! But Aaron's rod swallows their rods. "Yet Pharaoh's heart stiffened and he did not heed them."
E7:14-24 – **The ten plagues.** The plagues begin. Aaron strikes the waters of the Nile "in the sight of Pharaoh and his courtiers." The water – and in fact all the water throughout Egypt – is turned to blood. But the Egyptian magicians match this trick too.[46] So "Pharaoh's heart stiffened and he did not heed them."
E7:25-29 – After a week, Moses asks Pharaoh to let the Israelites go. If he doesn't, there will be a plague of frogs.

Exodus, Chapter 8
E8:1-3 – Aaron holds out his arm and rod over the waters of Egypt, "and the frogs came up and covered the land of Egypt." But the Egyptian magicians match this trick too.
E8:4-11 – Pharaoh is ready to let the Israelites go and make their sacrifice. Moses asks God to make the frogs go away, which he

---

[45] This is the first of several occasions on which God reveals that he is playing both sides of the street and that he views the entire conflict as an opportunity to demonstrate his power to control the affairs of human beings. Later generations have, of course, made Passover a celebration of freedom, but the concept was largely unknown in the ancient world. Indeed, the Israelites themselves had slaves.

[46] It's not clear to me how they did this, since all the water has already turned to blood.

does (but they remain only in the Nile). The frogs pile up in heaps, the land stinks, but when Pharaoh saw that "there was relief, he became stubborn and would not heed them."

E8:12-15 – God tells Moses to tell Aaron to hold out his rod and "strike the dust of the Earth, and it shall turn to lice throughout the land of Egypt." The Egyptian magicians can't match this trick and tell Pharaoh that "This is the finger of God!". But Pharaoh still won't let the Israelites go.

E8:16-20 – Moses tells Pharaoh that if he doesn't let the Israelites go, God will let loose swarms of insects[47]- except in the region of Goshen, where the Israelites live. Sure enough, swarms of insects ruin the land of Egypt.

E8:21-28 – Pharaoh tells Moses and Aaron that the Israelites can make their sacrifice, but "within the land." Moses replies that if they sacrifice something untouchable to the Egyptians in front of the Egyptians, they might be stoned to death, so they have to go three days into the wilderness. Pharaoh agrees and asks Moses to plead with God to call off the swarms of insects. Moses does so, but "Pharaoh became stubborn this time also."

<u>Exodus, Chapter 9</u>

E9:1-7 – This time Moses threatens Pharaoh with livestock pestilence (the plague will not affect the livestock of the Israelites). The Egyptian livestock die, but Pharaoh still won't let the Israelites go.

E9:8-12 – God tells Moses and Aaron to take handfuls of soot and

---

[47] JPS (p. 116, note *a-a*) says that in other versions, this phrase is translated as "wild beasts." The wide variance between the different translations shows how difficult it is to get at the exact meaning of what would seem to be fairly common words.

throw them skyward "in the sight of Pharaoh." The soot becomes "a fine dust all over the land of Egypt" and causes "an inflammation breaking out in boils on both man and beast..." Again God stiffens Pharaoh's heart.
E9:13-20 – God tells Moses to tell Pharaoh that "this time I will send all my plagues upon your person, and your courtiers, and your people, in order that you may know that there is none like me in the world."

God says that he could have killed all the Egyptians with pestilence but has spared them "in order to show you my power, and in order that my fame may resound throughout the world." Moses is to tell Pharaoh that the next plague will be a very heavy hail that will kill all the slaves and livestock left out in the open.
E9:22-26 – The hail comes, along with thunder and fire, except in the region of Goshen.
E9:27-35 – Pharaoh admits that "I and my people are in the wrong." He tells Moses to plead for the end of the hail. The hail ceases, but Pharaoh still won't let the Israelites go.

Exodus, Chapter 10

E10:1-6 – God tells Moses that he, God, has hardened Pharaoh's heart so that he could display his power, and future generations will recount how "I made a mockery of the Egyptians." Moses threatens a plague of locusts.
E10:7-20 – Pharaoh's courtiers are very upset: "Are you not yet aware that Egypt is lost?" Pharaoh summons Moses and Aaron and tells them to go and worship. But he won't let the Israelites' children go along. He sends Moses and Aaron away.

Egypt is hit with a huge plague of locusts, who eat up all the grass and fruit left by the hail. Nothing green is left in all of Egypt.

Pharaoh pleads with Moses and Aaron again. God causes a very strong wind to lift the locusts and hurl them into the Sea of Reeds.[48] Again, God stiffens Pharaoh's heart.
E10:21-23 – The next plague is darkness. It lasts three days. "People could not see one another...but all the Israelites enjoyed light in their dwellings."
E10:24-29 – Pharaoh tells Moses to go and worship - but to leave his flocks and herds behind. Moses says that this won't do, because the Israelites have to pick their own livestock for sacrifice. For the fourth time, God stiffens Pharaoh's heart. Pharaoh tells Moses to get out and make sure that he, Moses, doesn't lay eyes on Pharaoh again, "for the moment you look upon my face you shall die." Moses agrees: "I shall not see your face again!"

Exodus, Chapter 11
E11:1-2 – God tells Moses that there will be one more plague, after which Pharaoh will let the Israelites go. He tells Moses to tell the Israelites to borrow silver and gold objects from their neighbors.
E11:3 – The text notes that God "disposed the Egyptians favorably toward the people" and that "Moses himself was much esteemed in the land of Egypt."[49]
E11:4-10 – Moses says that God has said that he will kill the first-born of all the Egyptians, including the cattle. Once again, the text notes that "the Lord had stiffened the heart of Pharaoh."

Exodus, Chapter 12

---

[48] Traditionally (but incorrectly) "Red Sea" (JPS, p.120, note *a*).

[49] This is presumably why the Egyptians agreed to lend their valuable objects to the Israelites.

E12:1-20 – **Origin of the Passover ritual.** God tells Moses and Aaron to tell the Israelites to prepare a "passover offering"[50] – a lamb which they are to slaughter at twilight; its blood is to be put on the door posts of their houses. They are to roast and eat the meat with unleavened bread and bitter herbs. They are to eat it hurriedly, with their sandals on and "your staff in your hand."

This day is to be celebrated as a festival "throughout the ages." The Israelites are to remove all leaven from their houses and eat nothing leavened for seven days; anyone who disobeys will be cut off from the community.

E12:21-28 – Moses tells the Israelites what God has commanded, and they do it.

E12:29-32 – God kills all the Egyptians' first-born children and cattle. Pharaoh summons Moses and Aaron in the middle of the night, tells them to be gone, and asks them to bring a blessing upon him as well.

E12:33-36 – The Egyptian people are also eager for the Israelites to be gone. The Israelites have to depart in a hurry, so they take their unleavened dough along in bowls.[51] They also leave with the silver and gold they had "borrowed from the Egyptians...thus they stripped the Egyptians."

E12:37-42 – The Israelites - 600,000 of them, excluding children - journey to Succoth, where they bake their unleavened bread. They had been in Egypt 430 years to the day.

E12:43-51 – The law of the Passover offering: No foreigner may eat it. A slave can eat it if he has been circumcised. So can strangers, if

---

[50] Or "protective offering" (JPS, p.122).

[51] The traditional origin of the *matzo* – but note that earlier in the same chapter, the Israelites had already been commanded to eat unleavened bread.

they and all their males are circumcised.

E12:49 – "There shall be one law for the citizen and for the stranger who dwells among you."[52]

<u>Exodus, Chapter 13</u>

E13:1-2 – God lays claim to every first-born, man and beast, among the Israelites.

E13:3-8 – Moses repeats the instructions about eating unleavened bread for seven days and celebrating a festival on the seventh day.

E13:9 – "And this shall serve you as a sign on your hand and as a reminder on your forehead."[53]

E13:11-15 – Instructions as to which first-born animals (but no children) are to be sacrificed.

E13:16 – "And so it shall be as a sign upon your hand and as a symbol on your forehead that with the mighty hand the Lord freed us from Egypt."[54]

E13:17-18 – God thinks that the Israelites "may have a change of heart when they see war, and return to Egypt," so he leads them on a roundabout route through the wilderness at the Sea of Reeds.

E13:19 – Moses brings with him the bones of Joseph, according to

---

[52] This directive occurs several times in the Torah. From a modern perspective, it has been reinterpreted as a call for the protection of the rights of minorities. But *in context*, it is almost always clearly a mandate regarding the particular law or rule that is being articulated: the rule must be obeyed by both Israelites and strangers alike.

[53] This is the commandment that has resulted in *tefillin* - quite a leap, in my opinion. Reading the text yields no such instruction, and there is in fact no word or phrase - no antecedent, to use the appropriate grammatical terminology - to which "this" refers.

[54] See footnote 52. As with E13:9, there is no word or phrase to which "it" refers.

an oath that Joseph had extracted from the children of Israel.
E13:20-22 – God guides them as a pillar of cloud by day and a pillar of fire by night.

Exodus, Chapter 14
E14:1-4 – God tells Moses to tell the Israelites to turn back and encamp, so that the Egyptians will think they're lost. "Then I will stiffen Pharaoh's heart and he will pursue them, that I may gain glory through Pharaoh and all his host; and the Egyptians shall know that I am the Lord."
E14:5-9 – **The parting of the Red Sea.** Pharaoh is told that the Israelites have fled.[55] He has a "change of heart," and he and his army set out after them and overtake them near the sea.
E14:10-14 – The Israelites become "greatly afraid," but Moses assures them that God will deliver them.
E14:15-18 – God tells Moses to lift up his rod and hold his arm over the sea "and split it, so that the Israelites may march into the sea on dry ground. And I will stiffen the hearts of the Egyptians so that they go in after them; and I will gain glory through Pharaoh and all his warriors, his chariots and his horseman. Let the Egyptians know that I am Lord...."
E14:19-20 – The angel of God and pillar of cloud are between the Egyptians and the Israelites. "Thus there was the cloud with the darkness, and it cast a spell upon[56] the night," so that the Egyptians

[55] Note the subtle deception, which is not referred to anywhere in the text: all along, Moses has told Pharaoh that the Israelites want to go off into the wilderness and celebrate a festival – he never said they wanted to fly the coop!

[56] Alternate translation: "and it lit up" (JPS, p.128).

could not come near the Israelites.
E14:21-25 – Moses holds his arm out over the sea, and God drives back the sea "with a strong east wind all that night, and turned the sea into dry ground." The Israelites pass through. The Egyptians come in pursuit, and in the morning, God looks down "from a pillar of fire and cloud" and throws the Egyptian army into panic by locking the wheels of their chariots.
E14:26-30 – Moses holds his arm out over the sea, which returns to its normal state. The Egyptians flee, but "the Lord hurled the Egyptians into the sea." Pharaoh's entire army drowns; as a result, the people fear God and have faith in him and in Moses.

Exodus, Chapter 15
E15:1-20 – Moses sings a long poem of praise to God. Then Miriam the prophetess, Aaron's sister, along with all the women, dance and sing their praises of God.
E15:22-26 – The Israelites come upon some water, but they can't drink it because it's too bitter. God tells Moses to throw a piece of wood into the water, which then becomes sweet. God promises that if the Israelites diligently keep all his laws, "then I will not bring upon you any of the diseases that I brought upon the Egyptians, for I the Lord am your healer."

Exodus, Chapter 16
E16:1-12 – It's been six weeks since the Israelites left Egypt. The people are grumbling because they're hungry. God tells Moses that he, God, will "rain down bread for you from the sky," and each day the Israelites will go out and gather that day's portion. And on the sixth day, what they gather will turn out to be twice as much as their previous daily portion.

Moses tells the Israelites not to complain against him and

Aaron, because it is God who will feed them. God tells Moses that he's heard the Israelites' grumbling and they'll have their fill of both flesh and bread.

E16:13-20 – "In the evening quail appeared and covered the camp; in the morning there was the fall of dew about the camp." When the dew lifts, there's a fine, flaky substance like frost on the ground. Moses tells them that it's the bread that God has given them. One person from each tent shall gather one *omer*[57] for each individual in that tent.

E16:17-20 – The Israelites gather the flaky substance; some gather much, others little. Yet when they measure it, they have as much as they need to eat. Moses tells them not to leave any of it over until morning, but some ignore his directive, and the substance becomes "infested with maggots and stank. And Moses was angry with them."

E16:21-26 – The Israelites gather their food from God every morning. On the sixth day they gather twice as much, yet it doesn't spoil, because God wants them to have enough for the Sabbath without having to work.

E16:27-30 – Nevertheless, some of the people go out on the seventh day to gather, but they find nothing.

E16:31-35 – A description of *manna*: "it was like coriander seed, white, and it tasted like wafers[58] in honey." The Israelites eat it for 40 years, until they come to Canaan. Moses tells Aaron to put one *omer* of *manna* in a jar to be kept throughout the ages.

Exodus, Chapter 17

---

[57] About 3.7 quarts.

[58] The meaning of the Hebrew word is uncertain (JPS, p.134, note *d*).

E17:1-7 – The journey continues. The Israelites encamp at Rephidim. There's no water, and they start quarreling and complaining to Moses. God tells Moses that when they arrive at the rock at Horeb, Moses is to strike the rock with his rod, and water will issue from it. He does, and the people drink.
E17:8-16 – The Amalekites engage in battle with the Israelites at Rephidim. Moses tells Joshua that he, Moses, will go to the top of a hill with "the rod of God" in his hand during the battle.

When he holds up his hand, the Israelites prevail; when he lowers it, the Amalekites have the edge. Aaron and Hur hold Moses' hands up until the sun sets and Joshua overwhelms the Amalekites.

God tells Moses, "Inscribe this in a document as a reminder, and read it aloud to Joshua: 'I will utterly blot out the memory of Amalek from under the heavens!'"

<u>Exodus, Chapter 18</u>

E18:1-12 – Jethro, Moses' father-in-law, brings Moses' wife Zipporah and his sons to the encampment. Moses tells Jethro everything that has happened. Jethro rejoices. He brings sacrifices to God, and Aaron and all the elders partake of the meal.
E18:13-27 – Jethro notices how hard Moses is working, handling all of the Israelites' complaints and disputes. He's worried that Moses will wear himself out. He urges Moses to seek out honest, upright men and "set these over [the Israelites] as chiefs of thousands, hundreds, fifties, and tens, and let them judge the people at all times."

<u>Exodus, Chapter 19</u>

E19:1-6 – The Israelites encamp in the wilderness of Sinai. God tells Moses to tell the Israelites that "if you obey me faithfully and keep

my covenant, you shall be my treasured possession among all the peoples...you shall become a kingdom of priests and a holy nation."
E19:7-13 – Moses tells the Israelites what God has said, and they agree. God tells Moses that "I will continue in a thick cloud, in order that the people may hear when I speak with you and so trust ever after."

He also tells Moses to tell the people to wash their clothes and abstain from sex for two days, because on the third day, he's going to come down, "in the sight of all the people, on Mount Sinai." No one is to touch the mountain on pain of death, but when the ram's horn "sounds a long blast,[59] they may go up on the mountain."
E19:16-25 – On the third day, at dawn, "there was thunder, and lightning, and a dense cloud upon the mountain, and a very loud blast of the horn; and all the people who were in the camp trembled."

The Israelites take their places at the foot of the mountain. "Now Mount Sinai was all in smoke, for the Lord had come down upon it in fire; the smoke rose like the smoke of a kiln, and the whole mountain[60] trembled violently. The blare of the horn grew louder and louder. As Moses spoke, God entered him in thunder."

God comes down to the top of the mountain and calls Moses up. He tells Moses to go back down and come up again with Aaron. Moses then goes back down to the people and speaks to

---

[59] The meaning of the phrase translated as "sounds a long blast" is uncertain (JPS, p. 138, note *b-b*.).

[60] JPS (p. 139, note *c*) notes that "some Hebrew manuscripts and the Greek read, 'all the people.'" Once again, the wide disparity between the two translations illustrates the difficulty of getting at the original meaning of the Torah text.

them.

Exodus, Chapter 20

The Ten Commandments.

E20:2-3 – "I the Lord am your God who brought you out of the land of Egypt, the house of bondage: you shall have no other gods besides me."

E20:4-6 – Do not make or bow down to sculptured images, for "I the Lord your God am an impassioned God, visiting the guilt of the parents upon the children, upon the third and fourth generation of those who reject me, but showing kindness to the thousandth generation of those who love me and keep my commandments."

E20:7 – Do not take God's name in vain.

E20:8-11 – "Remember the Sabbath day and keep it holy."

E20:12 – Honor your father and mother.

E20:13 – "You shall not murder... commit adultery... steal...[or] bear false witness against your neighbor."

E20:14 – "You shall not covet...."

E20:15-18 – The thunder, lightning, blare of the horn, and smoking mountain terrify the people. Moses tells them, "Be not afraid; for God has come only in order to test you and in order that the fear of him may ever be with you, so that you do not go astray." The Israelites remain at a distance, while Moses approaches the cloud.

E20:19-23 – God issues a prohibition against making any gods of silver or gold, and he gives Moses instructions for building an altar.

Exodus, Chapter 21

E21:2-11 – Rules for buying and selling slaves, including rules for selling one's daughter into slavery.

E21:12-3 – Treatment of murder versus manslaughter.

E21:14 – Death penalty for first-degree murder.

E21:15 – Death penalty for striking one's parents.
E21:16 – Death penalty for kidnaping.
E21:17 – Death penalty for insulting one's parents.
E21:18 – Compensation for assault victims.
E21:20 – Penalties for beating or murdering slaves.
E21:22 – Penalties and compensation for injuring a pregnant woman and causing miscarriage ("eye for eye, tooth for tooth").
E21:26 – Penalties for injuring one's slaves.
E21:28 – Penalties and compensation when one is gored to death by an ox.
E21:33 – Penalties and compensation when an animal falls into a pit.
E21:35 – Penalties and compensation when a man's ox gores his neighbor's ox.
E21:37 – Penalties and compensation for stealing livestock.

Exodus, Chapter 22
E22:4 – Penalties and compensation for letting one's livestock graze in another's land.
E22:5 – Compensation for damage from fire that one has started.
E22:6ff – How to handle situations when goods loaned to another for safekeeping are stolen: "both parties shall come before God: he whom God declares guilty shall pay double to the other."
E22:9ff – How to handle situations when one man gives livestock to another to guard, and the animal dies, is injured or stolen with no witnesses.
E22:13 – Compensation for loaned livestock that is injured.
E22:15 – Penalties and compensation for seducing a virgin.
E22:17 – "You shall not tolerate a sorceress."
E22:18 – Death penalty for bestiality.

E22:19 – Condemnation of "whoever sacrifices to a god other than the Lord."
E22:20 – "You shall not wrong a stranger or oppress him, for you were strangers in the land of Egypt."
E22:21 – "You shall not ill-treat any widow or orphan" ("My anger will blaze forth and I will put you to the sword").
E22:24 – Prohibition against charging interest.
E22:25-6 – "If you take your neighbor's garment in pledge," you must return it before sunset. "In what else shall he sleep?"[61]
E22:27 – "You shall not revile God, nor put a curse upon the chieftain of your people."
E22:28 – God gets the Israelites' firstborn sons, as well as the "first yield" of their vats, cattle, and flocks.
E22:30 – "You shall be holy people to Me"; also, prohibition against eating carrion.

Exodus, Chapter 23

E23:1 – "You must not carry false rumors; you shall not join hands with the guilty to act as a malicious witness."
E23:2 – "You shall neither side with the mighty to do wrong – you shall not give perverse testimony in a dispute so as to pervert it in favor of the mighty – (E23:3) nor shall you show deference to a poor man in his dispute."
E23:4 – You must return your enemy's ox or ass if either is found wandering off.

---

[61] Rabbis may interpret this as a command to serve the needy. But on the face of it, it's simply about returning borrowed goods. If everyone is poor, you have to give the other person's garment back, because he doesn't have anything else to wear. Anyway, it's one of God's better moments: "...if he cries out to me, I will pay heed, for I am compassionate."

E23:5 – You must help your enemy if his ass is carrying too heavy a load.

E23:6 – "You shall not subvert the rights of your needy in their disputes."[62]

E23:7 – "Keep far from a false charge; do not bring death on those who are innocent and in the right..."

E23:8 – "Do not take bribes..."

E23:9 – Repeats E22:20.

E23:10 – Principles of agricultural land management.

E23:12 – Command to rest on the Sabbath.[63]

E23:13 – Don't even mention other gods.

E23:14 – Command to hold three festivals: the Feast of Unleavened Bread, the Feast of the Harvest, and the Feast of the Ingathering "at the end of the year, when you gather in the results of your work from the field."

E23:17 – "Three times a year all your males shall appear before the Lord."

E23:18 – Rules for making blood sacrifice.

E23:19 – God gets "the choice first fruits of your soil." Also, prohibition about boiling a kid in its mother's milk.

E23:20-33 – God promises to send an angel to guard the Israelites. He warns them against worshiping the gods of the peoples whose land he is going to give them. He promises blessings, fertility, and long life in exchange for loyalty. He tells the Israelites he's going to

---

[62] Sort of repeats E23:2.

[63] But interestingly enough, the reason given this time is that one's livestock and "bondman and the stranger may be refreshed." There's nothing about God and no reference to the creation story or to God's resting on the seventh day.

drive out the other peoples gradually so that the land will not become desolate. He warns them against making any covenants with the defeated peoples or their gods.

Exodus, Chapter 24

E24:1-4 – God tells Moses, along with Aaron, two other men and 70 elders, to come closer and bow low. Moses repeats all the commands and rules, the people agree to obey, and Moses writes them down.

E24:3-8 – Moses sets up an altar at the foot of the mountain and designates some young men to sacrifice bulls. He dashes some of the blood against the altar and reads the covenant aloud to the people.

E24:9-11 – Moses, Aaron, and the elders ascend the mountain and see God. Under God's feet "there was the likeness of a pavement of sapphire, like the very sky for purity."

E24:12-18 – God tells Moses to come up to him on the mountain and wait, and he'll give Moses stone tablets with his teachings and Commandments inscribed. Moses ascends, and the cloud covers the mountain and hides it for six days. On the seventh day, God calls to Moses from the midst of the cloud. The divine presence appears to the Israelites as a consuming fire on top of the mountain. Moses goes inside the cloud; he remains on the mountain 40 days and 40 nights.

Exodus, Chapter 25

Instructions from God to Moses regarding the gifts that the Israelites are to bring him; also, detailed instructions for the construction of the Ark, a table, and a lampstand of pure gold.

Exodus, Chapter 26

Instructions for building the Tabernacle and the curtain behind which the Ark is to be carried.

Exodus, Chapter 27
Instructions for building the altar and the enclosure of the Tabernacle. Also, instructions regarding the clear olive oil for kindling lamps which will burn "from evening to morning before the Lord. It shall be a due from the Israelites for all time throughout the ages."

Exodus, Chapter 28
Instructions for creating the priestly vestments, as well as two stones engraved with "the names of the sons of Israel," a breastplate, and other priestly accouterments.

Exodus, Chapter 29
Ritual instructions for ordaining priests, including the appropriate sacrifices.

Exodus, Chapter 30
E30:1-10 – Instructions for building an altar for burning incense; instructions for placement of the altar, burning incense, and purifying the altar.

E30:11-16 – God commands that each time a census is taken, a "ransom" shall be imposed on each Israelite "that no plague may come upon them through their being enrolled." The remainder of the chapter contains instructions on combining spices to make a sacred anointing oil, plus instructions for using the oil in the proper manner.

Exodus, Chapter 31

E31:1-11 – God tells Moses whom he has assigned to make the various items previously enumerated.

E31:14 – "You shall keep the Sabbath, for it is holy for you. He who profanes it shall be put to death: whoever does work on it, that person shall be cut off from among his kin."

E31:18 – God is finished speaking with Moses. He gives him the two tablets "inscribed with the finger of God."

Exodus, Chapter 32

E32:1-8 – **The Golden Calf.** The Israelites are impatient that Moses is taking so long. They ask Aaron to make them a God "who shall go before us, for that man Moses...we do not know what has happened to him." Aaron agrees and asks for the people's gold rings, which he makes into a calf. The people exclaim that this is the God who has brought them out of Egypt.

Aaron builds an altar and announces that "tomorrow's shall be a festival of the Lord!" The people offer sacrifices, then sit down to eat and drink, then rise to dance.[64] God tells Moses that he'd better hurry back, because the people have "been quick to turn aside from the way that I enjoined upon them."

E32:9 – God tells Moses, "'I see that this is a stiffnecked people...'" and is ready to let his "anger...blaze forth and...destroy" them. But Moses talks God out of destroying the Israelites. He argues that the Egyptians will say that God delivered the Israelites with evil intent

[64] While it seems amazing to the modern reader that Aaron goes along with the rebellion, the explanation has to do with the fact that the writer is supplying backstory for the political realities of the day. He (or she) wanted to besmirch the history of Aaron's priestly descendants and thus justify their lower status.

only to kill them off. He reminds God about his promises to the patriarchs. "And the Lord renounced the punishment he had planned to bring upon his people."

E32:15-20 – Moses comes down from the mountain. Joshua, who had gone partway with him, tells him he thinks he hears the cry of war in the camp, but Moses says it is "the sound of song." Moses sees the calf and the dancing, becomes enraged and hurls the tablets to the ground. He burns the calf, grinds it to powder, strews it upon the water, and makes the Israelites drink it.

E32:21-24 – Moses confronts Aaron: "What did this people do to you that you have brought such great sin upon them?" Aaron urges Moses not to be angry: "You know that this people is bent on evil." He says that they told him to make a god to lead them, and so he did.

E32:25-29 – "Moses saw that the people were out of control." He stands at the gate of the camp and says, "Whoever is for the Lord, come here!" The Levites rally to him. He tells them to go throughout the camp "and slay brother, neighbor, and kin." They kill 3,000 Israelites.

E32:30-35 – Moses admits to God that "this people is guilty of a great sin" and says that if God won't forgive them, he can "erase me from the record which you have written!" God tells him that this won't be necessary - but he does punish the Israelites with a plague.

Exodus, Chapter 33

E33:1-4 – God reiterates the promise he made to the patriarchs and enumerates the various tribes he's going to drive out; he promises the Israelites "a land flowing with milk and honey. But I will not go in your midst, since you are a stiffnecked people, lest I destroy

you on the way." The Israelites get very depressed at this and go into mourning; no one puts on "finery from Mount Horeb on."
E33:7-11 – Description of how Moses would enter the Tent of Meeting and speak to God, who takes the form of a pillar of cloud at the entrance of the tent.
E33:12-23 – Moses asks God to go in the lead, so that everyone will know that the Israelites have "gained your favor." God agrees. Moses asks if he can behold God's presence. God replies that no one can see his face and live. He tells Moses to station himself on a nearby rock "and, as my presence passes by, I will put you in a cleft of the rock and shield you with my hand until I have passed by." Moses will see his back but not his face.

Exodus, Chapter 34
E34:1-3 – God tells Moses to carve two new tablets of stone and to come to the top of the mountain alone.
E34:4-8 – Moses carves the tablets and goes up Mount Sinai. God passes before him and proclaims himself "compassionate and gracious, slow to anger, abounding in kindness and faithfulness, extending kindness to the thousandth generation, forgiving iniquity, transgression, and sin." Yet "he does not remit all punishment but visits the iniquity of parents upon children and children's children, upon the third and fourth generations."

Moses bows low and begs God to go in their midst, "even though this is a stiffnecked people."
E34:10-16 – God announces a covenant: "Before all your people I will work such wonders as have not been wrought on all the Earth or in any nation; and all the people who are with you shall see how awesome are the Lord's deeds which I will perform for you."

God then announces that he'll undertake ethnic cleansing; he promises to drive out six different tribes, and insists that the

Israelites, even though they may be tested to do so by the inhabitants of other lands, must not make any covenants with them: "No, you must tear down their altars, smash their pillars, and cut down their sacred posts."
E34:17 – "You shall not make molten gods for yourselves."
E34:18 – Command to observe the Feast of Unleavened Bread.
E34:19 – God again lays claim to "every first issue of the womb." "None shall appear before me empty-handed."
E34:21 – Command to observe the Sabbath.
E34:22 – Command to observe the Feast of Weeks and Feast of Ingathering. E34:23 – "three times a year all your males shall appear before the Sovereign Lord, the God of Israel."
E34:25 – A couple of rules on observing Passover.
E34:26 – Once again God lays claim to "the choice first fruits of your soil." Also repeats E23:19, the injunction against boiling a kid in its mother's milk.
E34:28 – Moses stays with the Lord for 40 days and 40 nights and writes down "on the tablets the terms of the covenant, the ten commandments."
E34:29-35 – Moses comes down from the mountain with two tablets. Aaron and the Israelites see that the skin of his face is radiant "and they shrank from coming near him." Moses tells them everything that God had told him. Then he puts a veil over his face. "Whenever Moses went in before the Lord to speak with him, he would leave the veil off until he came out." When he would tell the Israelites what God had commanded, they would see how radiant the skin of his face was. Then he'd put the veil back until he went to speak with God again.

<u>Exodus, Chapters 35-39</u>

Chapter 35 begins with Moses reminding the Israelites to keep the

Sabbath, on pain of death. Then Moses tells the Israelites to do everything that God said regarding the building of the Tabernacle and all its decorations.
These instructions go on for all of chapters 35, 36, 37, 38, and 39.
Exodus, Chapter 40 – More instructions for setting up the Tabernacle and the Tent of Meeting.
E40:20 – The Ark goes inside Tabernacle.

LEVITICUS

L1-3 – Instructions for making sacrifices in the correct manner.L3:16 – Dietary instructions: "All fat is the Lord's."
L3:17 – "It is a law for all time throughout the ages, in all your settlements: you must not eat any fat or any blood."

Leviticus, Chapter 4 – Procedures to follow when one person unwittingly incurs guilt in regard to any of the Lord's Commandments about things not to be done, and does one of them...". There are different rules for priests, for the whole community, for a chieftain, and for an individual person.

Leviticus, Chapter 5
L5:1-13 – Penalties for failing to testify, touching "any unclean thing," touching "human uncleanness," or "uttering an oath to bad or good purpose" (even though one doesn't recognize one's guilt at the time).
L5:14-19 – Penalties for breaking the Lord's Commandments.
L5:20 – Penalties for situations in which "one person sins and commits a trespass against the Lord by dealing deceitfully with his fellow in a matter of a deposit or pledge, or through robbery, or by

defrauding his fellow, or by finding something lost and lying about it"; what to do when one wants to "restore that which he got through robbery or fraud, or the deposit that was entrusted to him, or the lost thing that he found."

Leviticus, Chapters 6-9 – Instructions for the various kinds of sacrifices and burnt offerings.

Leviticus, Chapter 10 – God torches Aaron's son's ("fire came forth from the Lord and consumed them") because "they offered before the Lord alien fire, which he had not enjoined upon them."
L10:8-11 – God commands Aaron to "drink no wine or other intoxicant...when you enter the Tent of Meeting, that you may not die." He tells Aaron to distinguish "between the unclean and the unclean" and teach the Israelites all his laws.
L10:12-20 – More about the rules for sacrifice and where the sacrificial offering is to be eaten. Moses is angry with Aaron's two remaining sons because they did not eat the sacrificial offering in the right place.

Leviticus, Chapter 11 – **Dietary laws.** E.g., the Israelites may eat any land animal that has cleft hooves and chews cud. Of animals that live in water, they may eat only those that have fins and scales.

Leviticus, Chapter 12 – Rules concerning menstruation, purification and sacrificial offerings pertinent thereto.

Leviticus, Chapter 13 – Dermatological advice regarding leprosy and related matters. L13:45 – Lepers are required to call out "Unclean! Unclean!"

Leviticus Chapter 14 – "The ritual for a leper at the time that he is to be cleansed."
L14:34 – What to do when "I inflict an eruptive plague upon a house in the land you possess," i.e., Canaan.

Leviticus, Chapter 15 – Urological advice. E.g., "When any man has a discharge issuing from his member, he is unclean." Instructions for avoiding contamination and contagion. L15:16-17 – What to do when a man has "an emission of semen." L15:19ff – Gynecological advice and ritual. Who is clean and unclean, and under what conditions.

Leviticus, Chapter 16 – God dictates to Moses the ritual rules that Aaron must follow after the death of his two sons, whom God killed when "they drew too close to the presence of Lord"; God tells Moses what rituals Aaron must now practice. L16:29-30 – Command to observe Day of Atonement. "The Israelites must practice self-denial and "do no manner of work."

Leviticus, Chapter 17 – More rules for ritual sacrifice. L17:13-14 – Prohibition against eating blood.

Leviticus, Chapter 18
L18:2-5 – Prohibition against following any rules or laws but God's.
L18:6-20 – Rules for sexual conduct, e.g., "do not uncover the nakedness of your daughter-in-law: she is your son's wife; you shall not uncover her nakedness."
L18:21 – "Do not allow any of your offspring to be offered up to Molech."
L18:22 – "Do not lie with a male as one lies with a woman; it is an abhorrence."

L18:23 – Prohibition against bestiality.

Leviticus, Chapter 19

L19:2 – "You shall be holy, for I the Lord your God, am holy."
L19:3 – Honor your father and mother and keep the Sabbath.
L19:4 – No idols or molten gods.
L19:5-7 – Rules for sacrificial offerings.
L19:9-10 – Leave the gleanings of your harvest and the fallen fruit of your vineyard for the poor and the stranger.
L19:11 – Don't steal or "deal deceitfully or falsely with one another."
L19:12 – Don't take God's name in vain.
L19:13 – Prohibition against fraud or robbery. Also "the wages of a laborer shall not remain with you until morning."
L19:14 – "You shall not insult the deaf, or place a stumbling block before the blind."
L19:14 – "You shall fear your God: I am the Lord."
L19:15 – Show fairness to rich and poor alike; "judge your kinsman fairly."
L19:16 – "Do not deal basely[65] with your countryman. Do not profit by the blood of your fellow: I am the Lord."
L19:17 – "You shall not hate your kinsfolk in your heart. Reprove your kinsman but incur no guilt because of him."
L19:18 – "You shall not take vengeance or bear a grudge against your countryman. Love your fellow as yourself: I am the Lord."
L19:19 – Observe God's laws. Don't "let your cattle mate with a different kind" or sow your field with two kinds of seed or "put on cloth from a mixture of two kinds of material."
L19:20-22 – What to do if "a man has carnal relations with a woman

---

[65] The meaning of this phrase and of *profit by* are uncertain.

who is a slave and has been designated for another man, but has not been redeemed or given her freedom."

L19:23-25 – Wait five years before eating the fruit of any trees you plant.

L19:26 – Don't eat anything with its blood. Don't "practice divination or sooth saying."

L19:27 – "You shall not round off the side-growth on your head, or destroy the side-growth of your beard."

L19:28 – "You shall not make gashes in your flesh for the dead, or incise any marks on yourselves."

L19:29 – "Do not degrade your daughter and make her into a harlot, lest the land fall into harlotry and the land be filled with depravity."

L19:33-34 – Love the stranger as one of your citizens because you were strangers in the land of Egypt.

L19:35 – "You shall not falsify measures of length, weight, or capacity."

L19:36 – More on honest weights and standards.

L19:37 – "You shall faithfully observe all my laws of all my rules: I am the Lord."

<u>Leviticus, Chapter 20</u>

L20:1-6 – Penalties for anyone who "gives any of his offspring to Molech."

L20:7 – Repeats L19:2.

L20:8 – Repeats L19:37.

L20:9 – Death penalty for insulting your father or mother.

L20:10 – Death penalty for adultery.

L20:11 – "If a man lies with his father's wife...the two shall be put to death."

L20:12 – "If a man lies with his daughter-in-law, both of them shall

be put to death."
L20:13 – Death penalty for homosexual relations between men.
L20:14 – "If a man marries a woman and her mother, it is depravity, both he and they shall be put to the fire, that there be no depravity among you."
L20:15 – Death penalty for bestiality – both man and beast.
L20:16 – Same as above – both woman and beast.
L20:17 – Penalty for incest between brother and sister: excommunication "in the sight of their kinsfolk."
L20:18 – No sex during menstruation.
L20:19-21 – Prohibitions against incest with various family members.
L20:22-23 – Observe God's laws and not "the practices of the nation that I am driving out before you."
L20:25 – Separating the clean from the unclean.
L20:26 – "You shall be holy to me, for I the Lord am holy, and I have set you apart from other peoples to be mine."
L20:27 – Death penalty for "a man or woman who has a ghost or familiar spirit."[66]

<u>Leviticus, Chapter 21</u> – Instructions about how the priests, the (remaining) sons of Aaron, are to conduct themselves.
L21:1-6 – Prohibition against defiling oneself on account of a dead kinsman ("except for the relatives that are closest to [you]"). Priests "shall not shave smooth any part or their heads, or cut the side-growth of their beards, or make gashes in their flesh."
L21:7 – Priests may not "marry a woman defiled by harlotry, nor shall they marry one divorced from her husband."

---

[66] The meaning is unclear, but it may have something to do with divination (Hillman, p. 315).

L21:9 – Death penalty for the daughter of a priest who defiles herself through harlotry.
L21:10-15 – Rules of conduct for priests (they may marry only a woman who is a virgin).
L21:16-22 – Nobody with a physical defect is allowed to "offer the food of his God."

<u>Leviticus, Chapter 22</u>
More rules about who is allowed to partake "of any sacred donation that the Israelite people may consecrate to the Lord." Also, who may or may not "eat of the sacred donations." Animals offered for sacrifice must have no blemishes.

<u>Leviticus, Chapter 23</u>: "The fixed times of the Lord, which you shall proclaim as sacred occasions."
L23:3 – Observe the Sabbath.
L23:5ff – Rules for observing Passover.
L23:9-21 – Rules for the harvest sacrifice.
L23:22 – Leave grain for the poor.
L23:23-32 – Command to observe - and rules for observing - Rosh Hashana and the Day of Atonement.
L23:33ff – Command to observe the Feast of Booths. Rationale: to remind future generations that God made them live in booths during the exodus.

<u>Leviticus, Chapter 24</u>
L24:1-4 – Rules for setting up the kindling lamps outside the Tent of Meeting.
L24:5-9 – Rules for offering of bread and frankincense.
L24:10-16 – Story of a man who took God's name in vain. Penalty: death by stoning.

L24:17 – "If anyone kills any human being, he shall be put to death."
L24:18 – "One who kills a beast to shall make restitution for it: life for life."
L24:19-20 – "If anyone maims his fellow, as he has done so shall it be done to him: fracture for fracture, eye for eye, tooth for tooth."
L24:21 – Repeats L24:17 and L24:18.
L24:22 – "You shall have one standard for stranger and citizen alike."

Leviticus, Chapter 25
L25:2-7 – Instructions for observing, every seventh year, "a Sabbath of the Lord ... a year of complete rest for the land."
L25:8-13 – Command to observe, every 50th year, a "year of jubilee."[67] Instructions for buying and selling land in the year of jubilee.
L25:10 – "You shall proclaim release[68] throughout the land for all its inhabitants."
L25:17 – "Do not wrong one another, but fear your God: for I the Lord am your God."
L25:23 – "[T]he land must not be sold beyond reclaim, for the land is mine; you are but strangers resident with me."[69]
L25:25-28 – Legalities regarding recovery of the land sold to cover debts; special procedures in the jubilee year.

---

[67] The word comes from the Hebrew word *yobel*, "ram" or "ram's horn" (JPS, p. 237, note *b*).

[68] JPS (p. 237, note *a*) notes that others translate this word as "liberty."

[69] Inconsistent with the modern notion of private property.

L25:29-34 – Same as preceding verses, but with regard to real estate.
L25:35-37 – Rules for fair treatment of one's kinsmen: "do not exact from him advance or accrued interest, but fear your God."
L25:39-43 – Do not make a slave of your kinsman if he must live with you because he is in dire circumstances.
L25:44 – Addresses "[s]uch male and female slaves as you may have – it is from the nations round about you that you may acquire male and female slaves." The following verses contain more rules about the sale and possession of slaves.
L25:47-54 – Legalities regarding the right of redemption of one's kinsman who comes under the authority of "a resident alien among you."

Leviticus, Chapter 26
L26:1-2 – Don't make idols; keep God's Sabbath and venerate his sanctuary.
L26:3-13 – Benefits that the Israelites will receive if they obey God's commandments, e.g., "I will grant your rains in their season, so that the earth shall yield its produce and the trees of the field bear fruit...I will grant peace in the land, and you shall lie down untroubled by anyone."
L26:14-45 – Misfortunes that will befall the Israelites if they do not obey God's commandments, e.g., "You shall eat the flesh of your sons and the flesh of your daughters... I will spurn you. I will lay your cities in ruin and make your sanctuaries desolate, and I will not savor your pleasing odors. I will make the land desolate, so that your enemies who settle in it shall be appalled by it."

Leviticus, Chapter 27
Monetary values of the various items – animals, real estate, human beings – that are "vowed" or "consecrated" to God.

NUMBERS

Numbers, Chapters 1-2 – Census of the various tribes and clans.

Numbers, Chapter 3 – Lineage of Aaron and Moses; duties of the tribe of Levi; special status of Levites; the clans of the Levites and what their duties are. N3:38-50 – More about the Levites and how their firstborn children belong to God.

Numbers, Chapter 4 – Special status and duties of the Kohathite, Gershonite, and Merarite clans. Also, a census count of the various clans.

Numbers, Chapter 5
N5:2-4 – "Remove from camp anyone with an eruption or discharge and anyone defiled by a corpse."
N5:5-10 – Rules for making restitution for anyone who has committed a wrong and realized his guilt.
N5:11-31 – Ritual practices for situations in which either a woman has gone astray or her husband has "a fit of jealousy," whether or not she has actually defiled herself.[70]

Numbers, Chapter 6 – Ritual practices and obligations for nazarites.[71]

---

[70] Hillman points out (p. 362) that "the test displaced spiteful or vindictive husbands as judges and juries of their wives [and]... honored a broader dictum that the weak were to be protected against the arbitrary exercise of power by the strong."

[71] "Early exemplars of a holy life of separation and self discipline," Hillman, p. 362.

N6:22-27 – **The traditional three-part benediction**. Aaron and his sons are to bless the people of Israel by saying "the Lord bless you and protect you! The Lord deal kindly and graciously with you! The Lord bestow his favor upon you and grant peace!" God adds: "Thus they shall link my name with the people of Israel, and I will bless them."

<u>Numbers, Chapter 7</u> – All the various chieftains of Israel assemble; description of the tributes and offerings presented by each one.
N7:8-9 – How God speaks to Moses: when Moses is in the Tent of Meeting, he hears God's voice "addressing him from above the cover...on top of the Ark."

<u>Numbers, Chapter 8</u>
N8:1-4– God's instructions about the hammered gold lampstand, before which are to be placed seven lamps. Rest of Chapter 8 – God's directives regarding the special status and duties of the Levites.

<u>Numbers, Chapter 9</u>
N9:1-14 – Instructions for offering the Passover sacrifice, with special rules for those who are "unclean by reason of a corpse" and for "the stranger who resides with you."
N9:14 – With regard to Passover sacrifice, "there shall be one law for you, whether stranger or citizen of the country."
N9:15-23 – How God commands the Israelites to make and break camp, via the appearance of a cloud over the Tent of Meeting.

<u>Numbers, Chapter 10</u>

N10:1-10 – God tells Moses to make two silver trumpets, then tells him on what occasions they are to be sounded. "They shall be a reminder of you before your God: I, the Lord, am your God."
N10:11-28 – The desert journey continues. Description of what each tribe did to take down and reassemble the Tabernacle.

Numbers, Chapter 11
N11:1-3 – "The people took to complaining bitterly before the Lord. The Lord heard and was incensed: a fire of the Lord broke out against them, ravaging the outskirts of the camp. The people cried out to Moses. Moses prayed to the Lord, and the fire died down."
N11:4-9 – "The riff-raff in their midst felt a gluttonous craving," missing the good food they had in Egypt;[72] they're getting dissatisfied with the manna, even though "it tasted like rich cream."
N11:10-15 – The people are weeping,"the Lord was very angry, and Moses was distressed."
N11:16-20 – God tells Moses to gather 70 of Israel's elders and bring them to the Tent of Meeting, so that Moses doesn't have to bear his burden alone. God tells Moses that the Israelites will have meat for "a whole month, until it comes out of your nostrils and becomes loathsome to you."
N11:21-23 – Moses doubts that God can produce a whole month's worth of meat, but God answers, "Is there a limit to the Lord's power? You shall soon see whether what I have said happens to you or not!"
N11:31-34 – God creates a wind that sweeps quail from the sea and strews them "over the camp, about a day's journey on this side and one day's journey on that side...and some two cubits deep on the

---

[72] How Jewish!

ground." The people start to eat the meat, but "the meat was still between their teeth nor yet chewed, when the anger of the Lord blazed forth against the people and the Lord struck the people with a very severe plague."

<u>Numbers, Chapter 12:</u> God afflicts Miriam with a case of the scales because she and Aaron had spoken against Moses "because of the Cushite woman he had married." Moses prays to God to heal her, but he shuts her out of the camp for seven days,[73] after which time the Israelites push on.

<u>Numbers, Chapter 13:</u> God tells Moses to send scouts to check out "the land of Canaan, which I am giving to the Israelite people." After 40 days, they come back with the report that the land is indeed flowing with milk and honey, but "the people who inhabit the country are powerful, and the cities are fortified and very large."

The scouts (except Caleb) are intimidated, and they tell the other Israelites how formidable their enemy is: "we looked like grasshoppers to ourselves, and so we must look to them."

<u>Numbers, Chapter 14</u>

N14:1-2 – "The whole community broke into loud cries, and the people wept that night. All the Israelites railed against Moses and Aaron." Joshua and Caleb and the other scouts tell the Israelites not to worry, that God will give them the land as promised.

N14:10 – "As the whole community threatened to pelt them with stones, the presence of the Lord appeared in the Tent of Meeting to all the Israelites."

---

[73] The text doesn't say whether she was healed.

N14:11ff – God is really disappointed with the Israelites. After all the miracles he's performed, they still don't believe in him. He's also very angry. He's ready to "strike them with pestilence and disown them,"but Moses tells him that if he kills all the Israelites, people will think it was because he was unable to bring his people into the land he promised them. Moses begs God to pardon the Israelites, and God relents. BUT...
N14:21ff – God vows that no one who has "seen my presence and signs that I have performed in Egypt and in the wilderness...shall see the land that I promised on oath to their fathers; none of those who spurn me shall see it," except Caleb.
N14:26ff – God decides that nobody over the age of 20 is going to make it to the promised land. The Israelites are sentenced to 40 years of wandering: "You shall bear your punishment for 40 years, corresponding to the number of days...that you scouted the land: a year for each day. Thus you shall know what it means to thwart me. I the Lord have spoken: Thus will I do to all that wicked band that has banded together against me: in this very wilderness they shall die to the last man."
N14:36 – Special punishment for the scouts who returned and spread "calumnies about the land": they die of plague, "by the will of the Lord."
N14:39ff – The Israelites are overcome by grief and admit that they were wrong. Moses warns them against trying to attack the Amalekites and the Canaanites, but they do so anyway and are dealt "a shattering blow at Hormah."

Numbers, Chapter 15

Instructions for making a burnt offering or sacrifice and "producing an odor pleasing to the Lord."
N15:14 – Instructions for sacrificial ritual. Repetition of the

command that "there shall be one law for you and for the resident stranger."[74]

N15:17ff – God commands Moses to tell the Israelites that when they enter the promised land, they are to set aside, as a gift to the Lord, "the first yield of your baking."

N15:22-29 – Instructions for expiation "if you unwittingly fail to observe any one of the commandments that the Lord has declared to Moses." But anybody who "acts defiantly reviles the Lord" [and] "shall be cut off from among his people" (N15:30).

N15:32-36 – A man found gathering wood on the Sabbath is stoned to death.

N15:37-41 – Commandments to make and wear a fringed garment: "look at it and recall the commandments of the Lord and observe them, so that you do not to follow your heart and eyes in your lustful urge."

Numbers, Chapter 16

A group of 250 Israelites ("chieftains of the community"), motivated by Korah, Datham, Abiram, and On, rise up against Moses and Aaron for considering themselves holier than the rest of the people. Moses falls on his face.[75] Then he tells the group that the next morning "the Lord will make known who is...holy, and will grant him access to himself." He tells the group to burn some incense in fire pans, and we'll see whom the Lord chooses. "You have gone too far, sons of Levi!" Plus, Moses says, you are already

---

[74] In context, this has to do with the preceding instructions about sacrificial ritual. It doesn't say anything about morality, civics, politics, or protecting the rights of minorities – notions added by later commentators.

[75] JPS (p. 286, note *c*) suggests that another possible translation might be 'his face fell.'

set apart by being Levites, with special access to God, as well as other honors: "Do you seek the priesthood too?"[76]

N16:12-15 – Moses sends for Dathan and Abiram, two of the Israelites who instigated the uprising, but they refuse to come. Moses is very upset and tells the Lord to ignore their offering.

N16:16ff. – All 250 Israelites take their fire pans, put fire in them, lay incense on top, and take their places at the entrance of the Tent of Meeting. God appears and tells Moses and Aaron to stand back "that I may annihilate them in an instant."

N16:22 – "But they [fall] on their faces" and beg for mercy: "when one man sins, would you be wrathful with the whole community?"

N16:25ff. – Moses instructs the Israelites to move away from the three instigators.[77] He tells them that "if these men die as all men do, if their lot be the common fate of all mankind, it was not the Lord who sent me. But if Lord brings about something unheard-of, so that the ground opens its mouth and swallows them up with all that belongs to them...you shall know that these men have spurned the Lord."

N16:32 – The Earth opens up and swallows them up with their households and possessions.

N16:35 – "And a fire went forth from the Lord and consumed the 250 men offering the incense."

---

[76]Plaut (p. 1135) notes that "the distinction between ordinary Israelites, priests, and Levites had [probably] not yet hardened at the time of Korah's rebellion...but subsequently the boundaries between them were clearly defined. Two classes of guards now protected the sacred precincts from all outsiders: priests, who were the chief officers and who also had access to the inner court, and Levites, who worked under their command."

[77] The text mentions only three; we don't find out what happened to On.

Numbers, Chapter 17

N17:2 – God orders Aaron's son to remove the fire pans – "for they have become sacred" and hammer them into sheets as plating for the altar – and to "serve as a warning to the people of Israel."

N17:6 – "The next day the whole Israelite community railed against Moses and Aaron," because they had brought death upon the people.

N17:8 – God appears and tells Moses and Aaron to remove themselves from the community, "that I may annihilate them in an instant." Moses tells Aaron to take the fire pans, add incense, and "make expiation for them. For wrath has gone forth from the Lord: the plague has begun!"

N17:12 – Aaron makes expiation, and just in time too: 14,700 people die.

N17:16-20 – God tells Moses to take one staff from each chieftain and inscribe each man's name on it, then put it in the Tent of Meeting.

N17:20 – God says: "The staff of the man whom I choose shall sprout and I will rid myself of the incessant mutterings of the Israelites against you."

N17:23 – Moses finds that the staff of Aaron has sprouted, produced blossoms, and born almonds.

N17:25 – God tells Moses that this incident is to be "as a lesson to rebels, so that their mutterings against me may cease, lest they die."

N17:27 – The Israelites are really scared: "Lo, we perish! We are lost, all of us lost!"

Numbers, Chapter 18

Lots of directions from the Lord to Aaron, regarding the privileges and duties of the Levites.

N18:20 – "You shall, however, have no territorial share among them or own any portion in their midst; I am your portion and your share among the Israelites."

Numbers, Chapter 19

N19:1-10 – Rules for sacrificing a cow.

N19:11-22 – Additional hygienic rules: how to purify yourself if you touch a human corpse.

Numbers, Chapter 20

N20:1-11 – The Israelites complain about their lack of water. God appears to Moses and tells him to assemble the community; God says that Moses will get water out of a rock. Moses hits the rock, and out comes water.

N20:12-13 – But "because you did not trust me enough to affirm my sanctity in the sight of the Israelite people," Moses and Aaron are not going to reach the promised land.

N20:14-21 – An incident with the Edomites. They won't let the Israelites pass through, even though they're willing to pay their way. The Jews turn away from a fight.

N20:22-28 – Aaron dies atop Mount Hor.

Numbers, Chapter 21

N21:1-3 – The Israelites' first clash with the Canaanites. God hears their plea and delivers up the enemy.

N21:4-9 – The Israelites complain about food and water, God sends serpents who bite them, and many people die. People come to Moses, beg him to intercede and get rid of the serpents. He does.

Then God tells Moses to make a snake-like figure and "mount it on a standard. And if anyone who is bitten looks at it, he shall recover."

N21:10-20 – Account of the route that the Israelites take. God tells

Moses to gather the Israelites so that he can give them water. The Israelites sing a song, the meaning of at least some of which is, in the JPS editors' words, "no longer certain."
N21:21-25 – The Amorites refuse to allow the Israelites to pass.
N21:24 – "Israel put them to the sword, and took possession of their land..."

Remainder of Chapter 21 – Accounts of more Israelite victories. A poem celebrating them.

Numbers, Chapter 22

A story about how the king of Moab, "alarmed because that people [i.e., the Israelites] are so numerous," tries to get a man named Balaam to put a curse on the Israelites. God warns him against doing so, and he refuses.

The king's son Balak sends more dignitaries and promises rewards. Balaam asks the visitors to stay overnight so that he can speak with God. God comes to him and tells them that he can go with the king's son and dignitaries – but he must do whatever God commands. Following an incident in which his ass' path is blocked by an angel and God gives the ass power to speak, Balaam arrives and is greeted by Balak; he tells Balak that he, Balaam, can say only what God wants him to say.

Numbers, Chapter 23

More back-and-forth with God, Balak, and Balaam, who builds a number of altars, gets the king's son to give him seven bulls, and decides where he's going to do whatever it is that God wants him to do. (This chapter also includes two fairly obscure passages of verse.)

Numbers, Chapter 24

Balaam looks at the encampments of Israel and cannot curse them but blesses them – three times, in fact. His excuse is that whatever God says, he has to say. Then, as a parting shot, he tells Balak "what this people will do to your people in days to come." He dooms the Amalekites, Kenites, and several other peoples besides. N24:23 – "Alas, who can survive except God has willed it!"

Numbers, Chapter 25

N25:1-5 – "The people profane themselves by whoring with the Moabite women, who invited the [Israelites] to the sacrifices for their god." God gets very angry and orders the death of the ringleaders.

N25:6-9 – One of the Israelites brings a Midianite woman into his tent, whereupon Phinehas, Aaron's grandson, stabs them both to death with his spear. This stops the current plague, which has claimed 24,000 lives.

N25:10-18 – Because of Phinehas' action in spearing in the illicit lovers, God tells Moses that "I grant him my pact of friendship." He then tells Moses to "assail the Midianites and defeat them – for they assailed you by the trickery they practiced against you."[78]

Numbers, Chapter 26: God orders Moses to take a census of everyone over the age of 20 – "all Israelites able to bear arms." The rest of the chapter lists all the tribes and clans. There are just over 600,000 Israelites in all. N26:64-5 – None of the 600,000 were among the ones originally recorded in the wilderness of Sinai. As God had promised, they all died in the wilderness.

---

[78] It doesn't seem all that deceitful to me – the Israelites engaged in whoring and heresy quite willingly.

Numbers, Chapter 27

N27:1-11 – Several women, daughters of one man who died, beg Moses to allow them to inherit their father's property. Moses asks God. God agrees and provides several other rules for the inheritance of property.

N27:12ff. – God tells Moses to go up to the heights of Abarim and "view the land that I have given to the Israelite people." He tells Moses that "When you have seen it, you too shall be gathered to your kin, just as your brother Aaron was." God is still angry at Moses' disloyalty: "[I]n the wilderness of Zin, when the community was contentious, you disobeyed my command to uphold my sanctity in their sight by means of the water."

N27:15-23 – Moses asks God to appoint someone else to lead the community, and God designates Joshua. Moses "laid his hands upon him and commissioned him – as the Lord had spoken through Moses."

Numbers, Chapter 28

N28:1-2 – God tells Moses to "command the Israelite people and say to them: Be punctilious in presenting to me at stated times the offerings of food due me, as offerings by fire of pleasing odors to me."

The rest of the chapter delineates various sacrifices and rituals, including the Passover sacrifice and the command to eat unleavened bread for seven days. Also, a command to observe the Feast of Weeks.

Numbers, Chapter 29: More rituals, observances, and instructions for sacrifices. Command to refrain from work on the first day of the seventh month and the 10th day of the seventh month; on the latter occasion, Israelites are also to practice self-denial.

Numbers, Chapter 30

N30:3 – Command to keep one's vows, oaths, and self-imposed obligations.

N30:4-6 – A woman's self-imposed vows or obligations are subject to her father's approval while she is still in her father's household.

N30:7-9 – If she marries, her vows are subject to her husband's approval. N30:14 – "Every vow and every sworn obligation of self-denial may be upheld by her husband or annulled by her husband."

N30:10 – The above does not apply to a divorced woman.

Numbers, Chapter 31

N31:1-12 – God tells Moses to "avenge the Israelite people on the Midianites; then you shall be gathered to your kin." Moses collects an army of 12,000 – 1,000 men from each tribe. The Israelites attack and defeat the Midianites.

They bring their captives and booty to Moses, who is annoyed that his army spared all the women - even though they are the very ones "who, at the bidding of Balaam, induced the Israelites to trespass against the Lord"- i.e., have sex (after which they were struck by the plague). All the women who have had carnal relations are killed.

N31:19-24 – Instructions for cleansing and purifying after battle.

N31:25-54 – How the booty is divided among the Israelites.

Numbers, Chapter 32

N32:1-15 – Two cattle-owning tribes - the Reubenites and the Gadites - ask to be given the land west of the Jordan. Moses is very upset by their reluctance to invade along with the rest. He reminds them that a similar incident resulted in the Israelites' having to wander in the desert for 40 years.

N32:16-27 – The two tribes offer to go in first as shock-troops, leaving their flocks and children behind on the land that they wanted. Moses agrees and gives them the land of the Amorites, plus some other territory, which they then rebuild.

Numbers, Chapter 33
N33:1-48 – Long, involved account of the Israelites' routes and encampments.
N33:38ff – Aaron dies, at the age of 123, in the 40th year after the Israelites left Egypt.[79]
N33:50-56 – God tells Moses that the Israelites are to completely destroy the Canaanites and take their land. If they don't completely annihilate the enemy, "those whom you allow to remain shall be stings in your eyes and thorns in your sides, and they shall harass you in the land in which you live; so that I will do to you what I planned to do to them."

Numbers, Chapter 34: God gives Moses the boundaries of the territory he's going to give to the Israelites – also, the names of the tribal chieftains who are going to get the land.

Numbers, Chapter 35
N35:1-8 – God tells Moses about the lands he's assigning to the Levites.
N35:9-15 – God tells Moses that in the land of Canaan, "you shall provide yourselves with places to serve you as cities of refuge to which a manslayer who has killed a person unintentionally may flee...so that the manslayer may not die unless he has stood trial before the assembly."

---

[79] This second account of Aaron's death repeats the events of N20:28.

The rest of the chapter is concerned with legal procedures regarding murder:
N35:16-19 – If you hit anybody with an iron, stone, or wooden object and kill that person, you are a murderer and must be put to death.
N35:19 – "The blood avenger himself shall put the murderer to death."
N35:22-28 – If you kill someone unintentionally,"the assembly" will protect you and "restore [you] to the city of refuge to which [you] fled, and there...[you] shall remain until the death of the high priest who was anointed with the sacred oil." You can't leave the city of refuge, because the blood-avenger can then kill you with impunity.
N35:30 – "If anyone kills a person, the manslayer may be executed only on the evidence of witnesses; the testimony of a single witness against the person shall not suffice for sentence of death."
N35:31 – "You may not accept a ransom for the life of a murderer who is guilty of the capital crime; he must be put to death."
N35:32 – " You may not accept ransom in lieu of flight to a city of refuge..."
N35:33 –"You shall not pollute the land in which you live; for blood pollutes the land and the land can have no expiation for blood that is shed on it, except by the blood of him who shed it."[80]

Numbers, Chapter 36: The adjudication of an issue regarding what happens to the land holdings of a certain group of women when these women marry.

DEUTERONOMY

---

[80] On the face of it, this is simply a repetition of the command not to commit murder. I really don't think it's a statement about ecology.

Deuteronomy, Chapter 1

Moses gathers the Israelites together. It's almost the end of their 40 years of wandering. He addresses them. He shows them the land that God has promised them and tells them to go ahead and take it.

D1:9ff – But he says that "I cannot bear the burden of you up by myself... (D1:12) how can I bear unaided the trouble of you, and the burden, and the bickering!" He tells the Israelites to pick out tribal leaders to hear the disagreements of the people.

The rest of Chapter 1: Moses recounts the story of the scouts who came back with Canaan with discouraging reports, including the part about how God refused to allow any of "this evil generation" (D1:35) to set foot in the promised land.

He reminds them that they admitted that they stood "guilty before the Lord" but nevertheless decided to fight the Amorites. God had told Moses to warn them not to do it, since he wouldn't be with them. They marched anyway and were defeated. After the defeat (D1:45), "you wept before the Lord; but the Lord would not hear your cry or give ear to you."

Deuteronomy, Chapter 2

D2:1-6 – The Israelites pass through the territory of the descendants of Esau. God tells them not to provoke the inhabitants; he tells the Israelites that they must pay for everything they eat or drink.

D2:7 – "Indeed, the Lord your God has blessed you in all your undertakings. He has watched over your wandering through this great wilderness; the Lord your God has been with you these past 40 years: you have lacked nothing." [81]

---

[81] To me, it seems like a pretty strange assessment of the 40 years, considering the plagues and other depredations.

D2:8-20 – The Israelites move on to the territory of the Moabites. God says to leave them alone, because they are the descendants of Lot.
D2:24ff – God urges the Israelites to engage the Amorites in battle – although at first, the Israelites come with an offer of peace. King Sihon refuses, battle ensues, the Israelites win and capture booty.

Deuteronomy, Chapter 3
Story of how the Israelites defeat two Amorite kings.
D3:21 – Moses assures Joshua that what God has done to these two kings, he will do to all the kingdoms "into which you shall cross over."
D3:22 – "Do not fear them, for it is the Lord your God who will battle for you."
D3:23 to end of chapter – Moses begs God to let him cross over to the promised land, but God says, "Enough! Never speak to me of this matter again!" He tells Moses to go up on top of Mount Pisgah to look at the land he will never enter.

Deuteronomy, Chapter 4
D4:1-4 – Moses tells the Israelites to give heed to God's laws, not to add anything or take anything away, and he reminds them how God wiped out those who followed Baal-Peor.
D4:5-8 – Moses says that these laws will be "proof of your wisdom and discernment to other peoples who on hearing of all these laws will say, 'Surely, that great nation is a wise and discerning people.' For what great nation is there that has a God so close at hand as the Lord our God whenever we call upon Him? Or what great nation has laws and rules as perfect as all this Teaching that I set before you this day?"
D4:9ff. – Moses tells the Israelites to teach their children reverence

for God and his gift of the Ten Commandments, as well as additional rules and laws "for you to observe in the land that you are about to cross into and occupy." As follows: D4:15-18 – Moses tells them that since they've never seen God in any form, they are not to create "a sculptured image in any likeness whatever."
D4:19-20 – Don't worship the sun, the moon, or the stars; you are God's people.
D4:21-24 – Moses tells them that he's not going to cross the Jordan, so they had better not forget their covenant, "For the Lord your God is a consuming fire, an impassioned God."
D4:25-31 – More threats - and promises too. If they create any sculptured images, they're going to be wiped out and scattered "among the nations to which the Lord will drive you. There you will serve man-made gods of wood and stone, that cannot see or hear or smell." But if they seek God, he won't forget their covenant: "For the Lord your God is a compassionate God: he will not fail you nor will he let you perish."
D4:32-40 – Moses praises God: "has anything as grand as this ever happened, or has its like ever been known? Has any people heard the voice of a God speaking out of a fire, as you have, and survived? Or has any God ventured to go and take for himself one nation from the midst of another by prodigious acts, by signs and portents, by war, by a mighty hand and outstretched arm and awesome power, as the Lord your God did for you in Egypt before your very eyes?"... etc.
D4:41-43 – Moses sets aside three cities of refuge, to which someone who has committed involuntary manslaughter may flee.

Deuteronomy, Chapter 5

Moses summons all the Israelites and tells them to listen to and observe the laws and rules that he's going to proclaim.

D5:6-7 – I brought you out of the land of Egypt...you may have no other gods beside me.
D5:8ff – No sculptured images. God promises to visit guilt upon third and fourth generations but to show kindness to "the thousandth generation of those who love me and keep my commandments."
D5:11 –Don't swear falsely by the name of the Lord.
D5:12-15 – Keep the Sabbath.[82]
D5:16 – Honor your father and mother.
D5:17 – No murder, adultery, theft, or bearing of false witness.
D5:18 – Do not covet.
D5:19-24 – Moses reminds the Israelites that these were the words given by the Lord when they were too afraid of God's fiery presence on the mountain and told Moses to go listen "and then you tell us everything that the Lord our God tells you, and we will willingly do it."
Rest of chapter: Recounting of the interaction at Sinai and a warning to obey God's Commandments.

Deuteronomy, Chapter 6

Moses enjoins the Israelites to "obey God's laws." The chapter provides the Israelites with various kinds of motivation to do so. First, a couple of positive outcomes:
D6:1 –"to the end that you may long endure."
D6:3 –"that it may go well with you and that you may increase greatly [in] a land flowing with milk and honey."

---

[82] Again, no rationale is given except as a reminder to the Israelites that they were slaves in Egypt.

D6:4-8 – These verses contain the famous passage of the *Shema*[83], as well as repetition of the commandments that resulted in *tefillin* and *mezuzahs*.
D6:10-15 – Moses reminds the Israelites that God is going to give them "great and flourishing cities that you did not build" as well as a lot of other things that they didn't earn, so they had better not forget God and had better revere only him, "for the Lord your God in your midst is an impassioned God – lest the anger of the Lord your God blaze forth against you and he wipe you off the face of the earth."
D6:16-19 – Continues in the same vein: the Israelites are not to "try the Lord your God." They are to keep all of his commandments, decrees, and laws, so that "it may go well with you and that you may be able to possess the good land the Lord your God promised on oath to your fathers, and all your enemies may be driven out before you."
D6:20-25 – More of the same, tying it all together, linking it to posterity: When your children ask the meaning of all the decrees, laws and rules, tell them that God freed us from Egypt and gave us the land he promised. Then he commanded us to observe all these laws "for our lasting good and for our survival."

Deuteronomy, Chapter 7
D7:1-5 – Instructions for the ethnic cleansing of "the land that you are about to enter and possess...seven nations much larger than you...you must doom them to destruction: grant them no terms and give them no quarter...you shall tear down their altars, smash their pillars, cut down their sacred posts, and consign their images to the

---

[83] Which the JPS translates as "Hear O Israel, the Lord is our God, the Lord alone."

fire."

D7:6-8 – Moses says that the Lord chose Israel to be his treasured people, not because they're the most numerous ("indeed, you are the smallest of peoples") but "because the Lord favored you and kept the oath he made to your fathers" after freeing the Israelites from Egypt.

D7:9-11– Promises and threats: God "keeps his covenant faithfully to the thousandth generation of those who love him and keep his commandments, but...instantly requites with destruction those who reject him - never slow with those who reject him, but requiting them instantly."

D7:12-15 – More promises: fertility of womb and soil, freedom from sickness: "He will not bring upon you any of the dreadful diseases of Egypt, about which you know, but will inflict them upon all your enemies."

D7:16-26 (rest of chapter) – Destroy all the peoples that the Lord your God delivers to you, show them no pity, don't worship their gods ("for that would be a snare to you"). Don't be afraid of them; just remember what God did to Pharaoh and the Egyptians. "Thus will the Lord your God do to all the peoples you now fear." He'll also send a plague against them "until those who are left in hiding perish before you."

D7:25-26 – "Consign the images of their gods to the fire," and don't "covet the silver and gold on them and keep it for yourselves, lest you be ensnared thereby...you must reject it as abominable and abhorrent."

Deuteronomy, Chapter 8

D8:1-4 – God enjoins the Israelites to obey all his commandments.

D8:2 – Another reason for the 40 years of wandering: "that he might test you by hardships to learn what was in your hearts:

whether you would keep his commandments or not."
D8:3 – God has "subjected you to the hardship of hunger and then gave you *manna* to eat, which neither you nor your fathers had ever known, in order to teach you that man does not live on bread alone, but that man may live on anything that Lord decrees."
D8:7-10 – Description of the richness of the land that God is bringing the Israelites into.
D8:11-18 – Warning not to forget that God is responsible for all the good things that have happened to the Israelites: "beware lest your heart grow haughty...and you say to yourselves, 'My own power and the might of my own hand have won this wealth for me.' Remember that it is the Lord your God who gives you the power to get wealth...".
D8:19-20 – Another threat: "if you do forget the Lord your God and follow other gods to serve them or bow down to them, I warn you this day that you shall certainly perish."

<u>Deuteronomy, Chapter 9</u>
An apparently aggrieved Moses addresses the Israelites. He tells them that they are about to face the formidable Anakites and that "none other than the Lord your God is crossing at your head, a devouring fire; it is he who will wipe them out."
D9:7 – Moses makes it very clear that God is giving them the land not because of their virtues but because of the wickedness of the other nations. God is dispossessing those nations to fulfill the oath that he made to Abraham, Isaac, and Jacob.

Moses reminds them that they are a stiffnecked people, that they provoked God to anger in the wilderness, and in fact "from the day that you have left the land of Egypt until you reach this place, you have continued defiant toward the Lord."[84]

Moses recounts the entire incident of the golden calf. He says that God told him, "I see that this is a stiffnecked people. Let me alone and I will destroy them and blot out their name from under heaven, and I will make you a nation far more numerous than they."

Moses retells the story of how he smashed the tablets, fasted for 40 days and 40 nights, destroyed the golden calf by grinding up and throwing its dust into the stream - and interceded for Aaron as well.

D9:22-23 – Moses recounts other occasions on which "you provoked the Lord... you flouted the command of the Lord your God; you did not put your trust in him and did not obey him." In fact (D9:24), "As long as I have known you, you have been defiant toward the Lord."

D9:25-29 – Moses recounts his earlier conversation (N14:11ff), in which he persuaded God not to destroy the Israelites because others might think "the Lord was powerless to bring them into the land that he promised them...Yet they are your very own people whom you freed with your great might and your outstretched arm."

Deuteronomy, Chapter 10: Moses continues his reminiscences. Verses 1 through 10 recount how God told Moses to carve two new tablets out of stone and build a wooden ark. God "inscribed on the tablets the same text as on the first, the Ten Commandments that he

---

[84] This seems to be something of an overstatement. The entire preceding text of the Torah, while it does recount occasions on which the Israelites disobeyed or lost their nerve, is not a chronicle of continued defiance.

addressed to you on the mountain out of the fire on the day of the Assembly." Moses also recounts the death of Aaron and the assignment by God of special status to the Levites.

Moses continues: After another 40 days and 40 nights on the mountain, God agreed not to destroy the Israelites and told me to resume the march. And after all this, God asks only that "you revere him, love him and serve him "with all your heart and soul, keeping the Lord's Commandments and laws...for your good."

Moses notes that God possesses the entire universe, and yet he was drawn to "your fathers...so that he chose you, their lineal descendants, from among all peoples...Cut away, therefore, the thickening about your hearts and stiffen your necks no more."

Deuteronomy, Chapter 11

Continues in the same vein as the previous chapter: recounts all the things that God did for the Israelites and enjoins them to keep all of his commandments so that they can enter and take possession of the promised land and long endure there, as God promised their fathers.

D11:10-12 – Description of how beautiful the Promised Land is, compared to Egypt.

D11:13-17 – More promises and threats, e.g., "You shall gather in your new grain and wine and oil. I will also provide grass in the fields for your cattle and thus you shall eat your fill. Take care not to be lured away to serve other gods and bow to them. For the Lord's anger will flare up against you and you will soon perish."

D11:18-21 – Repeats D4:8: Remember God's words by binding them as a sign on your hand and forehead, teaching them to your children, and inscribing them on your door posts.

D11:22-25 – More of the same: if you keep God's laws, he will "dispossess nations greater and more numerous than you," and

your territory shall extend "from the wilderness to the Lebanon" and from the Euphrates River to the Mediterranean Sea.
D11:25 – "No man shall stand up to you: the Lord your God will put the dread and the fear of you over the whole land in which you set foot...".

Deuteronomy, Chapter 12
D12:1 – "These are the laws and rules that you must carefully observe in the land that the Lord...is giving you to possess, as long as you live on earth."

The rest of the chapter elaborates: Destroy all of the other nations' worship sites, "tear down their altars, smash their pillars, put their sacred posts to the fire...". Make sacrifices, tithes, contributions, and other "votive offerings" only in the places that God designates. Don't eat the blood of the animals you slaughter.
D12:29-31 – Do not inquire into or attempt to practice the religion of the nations whose land God has given you (D12:31 – "they even offer up their sons and daughters in fire to their gods").

Deuteronomy, Chapter 13
D13:2-6 – "If there appears among you a prophet or a dream-diviner and he gives you a sign or portent, saying, 'Let us follow and worship another god'" don't do it, even "if a sign or portent that he named to you comes true."
D13:6 – "As for that prophet or dream-diviner, he shall be put to death."
D13:7-12 – Even if your wife or brother urges you to worship another god, don't do it. "Show him no pity or compassion, and do not shield him; but take his life" by stoning.
D13:13-19 – The same harsh punishments for any Israelites who "[subvert] the inhabitants of their town" and persuade them to

worship other gods: "Doom [the town] and all that is in it to destruction...Let nothing that has been doomed stick to your hand in order that the Lord may turn from his blazing anger and show you compassion, and in compassion increase you as he promised your fathers on oath...."

Deuteronomy, Chapter 14

Entire chapter consists of moral and ritual directives:
D14:1 – "You shall not gash yourselves or shave the front of your heads because of the dead."
D14:2 – Reference to Israelites as God's chosen people.
D14:3-21 – The familiar dietary laws – animals, birds, and marine life that may and may not be eaten – plus some not-so-familiar ones, e.g., "You shall not eat anything that has died a natural death."
D14:22-26 – Instructions to consume their bounty in a place which God chooses (or, if it's too far, to convert it to cash, then spend the money "on anything you want – cattle, sheep, wine or other intoxicant, or anything you may desire").[85]
D14: 27-29 – Instructions for contributions to the Levites, who don't have any hereditary land.

Deuteronomy, Chapter 15

D15:1-3 – Instructions to practice, every seventh year, forgiveness of debts. "You may dun the foreigner; but you must remit whatever is due you from your kinsman."
D15:4-5 – If you only heed the Lord, there will be no needy among you.

---

[85] This is the only time in the entire Torah that God actually tells the Israelites to go out and have a good time!

D15:6 – "For the Lord your God will bless you as he has promised you: you will extend loans to many nations, but require none yourself; you will dominate many nations, but they will not dominate you."
D15:7-10 – If there is a needy person among you, you must be generous to him, even if the year of remission is approaching.
D15:10 – "Give to him readily and have no regrets when you do so, for in return the Lord your God will bless you in all your efforts and other undertakings."
D15:11 – "For there will never cease to be needy ones in your land, which is why I command you, open your hand to the poor and needy kinsman in your land."
D15:12-18 – Rules for freeing one's slaves. D15:16-17 – If the slave wants to remain in your household, "you shall take an awl and put it through his ear into the door, and he shall become your slave in perpetuity."
D15:19-23 – Rules for consecrating to God the firstborn of the flock.

Deuteronomy, Chapter 16
D16:1-8 – Instructions for observing Passover: no consumption of leaven; slaughtering the Passover sacrifice.
D16:9-17 – Instructions for observing the Feast of Weeks and the Feast of Booths. On these occasions, "all your males shall appear before the Lord your God in a place that he will choose. They shall not appear before the Lord empty-handed, but each with his own gift...".
D16:18-20 – Instructions to appoint magistrates and officials to "govern the people with due justice."
D16:19 – "You shall not judge unfairly: you shall show no partiality; you shall not take bribes, for bribes blind the eyes of the discerning and upset the plea of the just."

D16:20: "Justice, justice shall you pursue, that you may thrive and occupy the land of the Lord your God is giving you."
D16:21 – Don't set up a sacred post near God's altar.

Deuteronomy, Chapter 17
D17:1 – Don't sacrifice an ox or sheep that has any serious defect.
D17:2-7 – Procedures for rooting out worshipers of other gods and punishing them by stoning them to death. "Thus you will sweep out evil from your midst."
D17:8-13 – Procedures for handing over cases that are "too baffling for you to decide, be it a controversy over homicide, civil law, or assault" to "the levitical priests, or the magistrate in charge at the time." The priestly verdict is binding, under penalty of death: "Thus you will sweep out evil from Israel: all the people who hear will be afraid and will not act presumptuously again."
D17:14-17 – If you want to have a king, it's OK with God, as long as God gets to choose the king. Make sure it's not a foreigner, and make sure that he doesn't "keep many horses or send people to Egypt to add to his horses, since the Lord has warned you, 'You must not go back that way again.' And he shall not have many wives lest his heart go astray, nor shall he amass silver and gold to excess."
D17:18-20 – The king is to have a copy of "this Teaching" on a scroll, so that he can observe it faithfully, "to the end that he and his descendants may reign long in the midst of Israel."

Deuteronomy, Chapter 18
D18:1-5 – Required donations to the tribe of Levi, the priestly class, e.g., special parts of each animal sacrificed.
D18:6-7 – Levites who go somewhere else ("to the place that the Lord has chosen") are still due their required portions and

donations.

D18:9-14 – Do not imitate "the abhorrent practices" of the nations whose land God gives you, e.g., soothsaying, sorcery, spellcasting, "inquiries of the dead."

D18:15-22 – "[T]he Lord your God will raise up for you a prophet from among your own people, like myself [i.e., Moses]." God will do this because the Israelites had asked it of him at Horeb. Furthermore, they are to put to death any false prophets, i.e., those whose prophecies do not come true, because they do not speak for God.

Deuteronomy, Chapter 19

D19:1-7 – Instructions to set aside three cities of refuge for a person who kills another unwittingly. Three cities are prescribed so that the accidental killer can reach one of them quickly.

D19:8-10 – The Israelites can add three more cities "when the Lord your God enlarges your territory, as he swore to their fathers."

D19:11-13 – Death penalty for premeditated murder, penalty to be administered by the "blood-avenger."

D19:14 – Don't move "your countryman's landmarks, set up by previous generations."

D19:15 – "[A] case can be valid only on the testimony of two witnesses or more."[86] Repeats 17:6.

D19:16-21 – Cases of suspected false testimony are to be submitted to magistrates, who will decide the truth of the matter. If a person is deemed to have testified falsely, "you shall do to him as he schemed to do to his fellow...Nor must you show pity: life for life,

---

[86] Or perhaps three: JPS notes that the meaning is uncertain; the phrase may literally mean "three" (p. 367, note *a*).

eye for eye, tooth for tooth, hand for hand, foot for foot."

Deuteronomy, Chapter 20

D20:1-9 – Psychological preparations for battle. Officials are to speak to the troops before the generals take over.

First of all, have no fear, because the Lord your God is with you, even if the enemy's forces are larger than yours. Those who are to be sent back home: anyone who has built a new house but not dedicated it; planted vineyards but never harvested; paid the bride-price for his wife but not married her. These individuals are to finish their tasks, lest they die in battle and someone else harvest their vineyard or marry their proposed bride. Also, if anyone is afraid and disheartened, he should go back home, "lest the courage of his comrades flag like his."

D20:10-18 – When you approach a town to attack it, offer terms of peace. If the inhabitants surrender, they "shall serve you at forced labor." If they don't surrender, lay siege, kill all of the males, and take everything else as your booty. The preceding applies to distant towns that "do not belong to nations hereabout." But if the towns are in territories that God has given you – the lands of the Hittites, Amorites and Canaanites – "you shall not let a soul remain alive...lest they lead you into doing all the abhorrent things that they have done for their gods."

D20:19-20 – If you have to lay siege to a city, don't destroy its trees (except those that do not yield food).

Deuteronomy, Chapter 21

D21:1-9 – Ritual to be performed by the elders and magistrates to absolve the Israelites of blood-guilt if "someone slain is found lying in the open, the identity of the slayer not being known." (Involves the sacrifice of a heifer that has never been worked.)

D21:10-14 – Rules for what to do if one of your captives is a beautiful woman whom you want to marry. You have to keep her for a month in your house, but "after that you may come to her and possess her, and she shall be your wife." But if you don't want her anymore, you have to release her; you can't sell her or make a slave of her.

D21:15-17 – If you have two wives, "one loved and the other unloved," and the latter gives you your firstborn son, you still have to accept him and give him his birthright.

D21:18-21 – A wayward and defiant son who does not obey his parents even after they discipline him shall be brought to a public place and stoned to death. "Thus you will sweep out evil from your midst: all Israel will hear and be afraid."

D21:22-23 – If a man is guilty of a capital offense, executed, and impaled on a stake, the corpse cannot remain on the stake overnight; it must be buried the same day.

Deuteronomy, Chapter 22

D22:1-3 – You must try to return missing items, such as an ox or sheep gone astray, or a garment or "anything that your fellow loses and you find: you must not remain indifferent."

D22:4 – "If you see your fellow's ass or ox fallen on the road, do not ignore it; you must help him raise it."

D22:5 – Prohibition against transvestitism. Whoever wears the clothes of the other gender "is abhorrent to the Lord your God."

D22:6-7 – If you find a bird's nest with the mother sitting on the eggs or guarding the fledglings, "let the mother go, and take only the young, in order that you may fare well and have a long life."

D22:8 – When you build a new house, make a parapet for the roof, "so that you do not bring blood guilt on your house if anyone should fall from it."

D22:9 – Don't sow your vineyard with two different kinds of seeds.
D22:10 – Don't plow with an ox and an ass together.
D22:11 – Don't wear cloth that combines wool and linen.
D22:12 – Put tassels on the four corners of your garment.
D22:13-20 – Procedures for establishing the virginity of a woman whose husband becomes dissatisfied with her and claims she wasn't a virgin (involves producing the bloody cloth for the elders of the town). If the man is wrong, he is fined and flogged - and can never divorce the woman.
D22:20-21 – If he's right and she's not a virgin, she is to be stoned to death.
D22:22 – Death penalty for adultery (both participants).
D22:23-28 – If a man has sex with a betrothed virgin while she's in her town, both are to be stoned to death (because she didn't cry for help). However, if the rape occurs in the open country, "only the man who lay with her shall die." Also, a man who rapes a virgin who is not engaged has to pay the girl's father 50 silver shekels and marry her; he can never divorce her.

Deuteronomy, Chapter 23
D23:1 – "No man shall marry his father's former wife..."
D23:2 – "No one whose testes are crushed or whose member is cut off shall be admitted to the congregation of the Lord."
D23:3 – No *mamzer*[87] shall be admitted into the congregation of the Lord, not even to the 10th generation.
D23:4-7 – No Ammonite or Moabite shall be admitted into the congregation of the Lord, not even to the 10th generation, because

[87] The meaning of the Hebrew word is uncertain, although in Jewish law, it refers to the offspring of adultery or incest between Jews (JPS, note 3, p. 377).

"they did not meet you with food and water on your journey after you left Egypt, and because they hired Balaam to curse you." D23:6 – "But the Lord your God refused to heed Balaam...[and] turned the curse into a blessing for you...". D23:7 – "You shall never concern yourself with their welfare or benefit as long as you live."[88]

D23:8-9 – Don't abhor either Edomite...[your kinsman] or Egyptians, for you were a stranger in their land. Their children may be admitted to the congregation in the third generation.[89]

D23:10-15 – Instructions for conduct "when you go out as a troop against your enemies." Anyone who has had a nocturnal emission must leave the camp, bathe, and return only at sundown. D13-14 – Instructions for building a field latrine. D23:15-"Since the Lord your God moves about in your camp to protect you and deliver your enemies to you, let your camp be holy."

D23:16-17 – "You shall not turn over to his master a slave who seeks refuge with you from his master." He can live with you anywhere he chooses and must not be ill-treated.

D23:18-19 – Prohibition against "cult prostitution" by both men and women.

D23:20-21 – Prohibition against deducting interest from loans to your countryman. However, it's OK to deduct interest from loans to foreigners.

D23:22-24 – When you make a promise to God, you must fulfill it.

D24:25-26 – When you enter another man's vineyard or grain field, you can eat as much as you want to, but don't collect any and take it with you.

---

[88] Contradicts earlier directives about one law for Israelites and strangers alike.

[89] I.e., of residence in Israel's territory; JPS, p. 378, note *c*.

Deuteronomy, Chapter 24

D24:1-4 – If a husband divorces his wife and she marries someone else, but the second husband divorces her or dies, the first husband can't marry her again.

D24:5 – A man who gets married gets a one-year exemption from military service "to give happiness to the woman he has married."

D24:6 – "A hand mill or an upper millstone shall not be taken in pawn, for that would be taking someone's life in pawn."

D24:7 – Death penalty for kidnaping "a fellow Israelite, enslaving or selling him."

D24:8-9 – If someone gets a skin disease, "be most careful to do exactly as the levitical priests instruct you."

D24:10-13 – "When you make loans of any sort to your countryman, you must not enter his house to seize his pledge" [presumably a garment; see what follows]. D24:12: – "If he is a needy man, you shall not go to sleep in his pledge; [D24:13 –] you must return the pledge to him at sundown, that he may sleep in his cloth and bless you...".

D24:14-15 – Don't abuse a needy and destitute laborer, whether an Israelite or not. D24:15 – "You must pay [the laborer] his wages on the same day, before the sun sets, for he is needy and urgently depends on it; else he will cry to the Lord against you and you will incur guilt."

D24:16 – "Parents shall not be put to death for children, nor children be put to death for parents: a person shall be put to death only for his own crime."

D24:17 – "You shall not subvert the rights of the stranger or the fatherless; you shall not take a widow's garment in pawn."

D24:19 – When you reap your harvest and overlook a sheaf, don't go back to get it. It goes to "the stranger, the fatherless, and the widow."

D24:20-21 – The same thing applies to the fruit of your olive trees and the grapes of your vineyard.

Deuteronomy, Chapter 25

D25:1-3 – A man who is found guilty in a dispute and condemned to flogging must be given 40 lashes but no more, "lest being flogged further, to excess, your brother be degraded before your eyes."
D25:4 – "You shall not muzzle an ox while it is threshing."
D25:5-10 – If two brothers are living together and one of them dies and leaves no son, the surviving brother gets to take his wife as his own until she has a son, "that his name may not be blotted out in Israel." But if he doesn't want to marry his brother's widow, even after the elders of the town have tried to persuade him to do so, then "his brother's widow shall go up to him in the presence of the elders, pull the sandal off his foot, spit in his face, and make this declaration: Thus shall be done to the man who will not build up his brother's house! [D25:1 –] And he shall go in Israel by the name of 'the family of unsandaled one.'"
D25:11-12 – "If two men get into a fight with each other, and the wife of one comes up to save her husband from his antagonist and puts out her hand and seizes him by the genitals, you shall cut off her hand; show no pity."
D25:13-16 – Injunction to practice honest weights and measures.
D25:17-19 – Never forget how the Amalekites surprise-attacked you "when you were famished and weary."

Deuteronomy, Chapter 26: Chapter begins with a list of ritual instructions: give God the first fruit of the land you settle in; recount the Exodus story as you do so; and give portions to the Levites, the stranger, the fatherless, and the widow; ask for God's blessing.

The rest of the chapter (D26:16-19) is an exchange of affirmations: the Jews affirm that they will obey God, and God affirms that they are "his treasured people who shall observe all his commandments, and that he will set you, in fame and renown and glory, high above all the nations that he has made..."

Deuteronomy, Chapter 27

D27:1-3 – Moses and the elders of Israel tell the people that as soon as they've crossed the Jordan, they're to set up large stones, coat them with plaster, and inscribe upon them all the words of "this Teaching."

D27:5-8 – Instructions to build an altar, make a sacrifice, rejoice, and inscribe every word "most distinctly."

D27:11-26 – The ritual of the curses and the blessings. Moses gives instructions for splitting the Israelites into two groups of six tribes each after they've crossed the Jordan.

Each group is to stand on a different mountain. One group is to stand on Mount Gerizim "when the blessing for the people is spoken" [follows in Chapter 28]. The other group stands on Mount Ebal for the curses, which the Levites "shall then proclaim in a loud voice to all the people of Israel."

The following are cursed: anyone who makes "a sculptured or molten image, abhorred by the Lord;" insults his parents; "moves his fellow countryman's landmark;" "misdirects the blind person on his way"; "subvertsthe rights of the stranger, the fatherless, and the widow"; commits incest or bestiality; "strikes down his fellow countryman in secret"; "accepts a bribe in the case of the murder of an innocent person;"[90] or will not accept "the

[90] The JPS version explains (p. 385) that this bribe would be offered to acquit the murderer. But the JPS also notes that others interpret this passage

terms of this Teaching."

Deuteronomy, Chapter 28

Chapter begins with the blessings that the Israelites will enjoy if they obey God's Commandments.

Some of the blessings are material: "Blessed shall be the issue of your womb, the produce of your soil" (D20:4); also, military victory (D28:7).

Some are general: "Blessed shall you be in your comings and blessed shall you be in your goings" (D28:6).

Some are metaphorical: "Blessed shall be your basket..." (D28:5).

D28:12 – Repeats the prediction that "you will be creditor to many nations, but debtor to none."

D28:13 promises supremacy: "the Lord will make you the head, not the tail; you will always be at the top and never at the bottom..."

The rest of the chapter is a litany of curses and horrors that makes the previous one in Leviticus seemed tepid. This one goes on for 52 verses. It reverses all the blessings just given and then presents a long list of threats that are far more rich and detailed than the blessings, graphic to the point of ghastliness, e.g., D28:56-58 – "And she who is most tender and dainty among you, so tender and dainty that she would never venture to set foot on the ground, shall begrudge the husband of her bosom, and her son and her daughter, the afterbirth that issues from between her legs and the babies she bears; she shall eat them secretly, because of her want, in the desperate straits to which your enemy shall reduce you in your towns."

Or: "the Lord will inflict extraordinary plagues upon you

---

as meaning "accepts a bribe to slay an innocent person."

and your offspring, strange and lasting plagues, malignant and chronic diseases (D28:59-60)."

Or: "The life you face shall be precarious; you shall be in terror, night and day, with no assurance of survival" (D28:66).

Deuteronomy, Chapter 29: This chapter begins Moses' final peroration.

Moses begins by reminding the Israelites about their 40-year trek (during which, miraculously, "the clothes on your back did not wear out, nor did the sandals on your feet"). He notes that God has performed many "wondrous feats...Yet to this day the Lord has not given you a mind to understand or eyes to see or ears to hear."

He reminds them of the covenant "which the Lord your God is concluding with you this day." He warns against being tempted by the gods of the nations they've encountered (D29:16 – "the detestable things and the fetishes of wood and stone, silver and gold, that they keep").

Most of the rest of the chapter is concerned with the vile things that God will do to those who are so tempted (D29:21-22 – "...plagues and diseases...soil devastated by sulfur and salt, beyond sowing and producing..."). The chapter ends with a description of how these people will be viewed by future generations, including D29:27 – "The Lord uprooted them from their soil in anger, fury and great wrath and cast them into another land, as is still the case."

Chapter concludes with "Concealed acts concern the Lord our God; but with overt acts, it is for us and our children ever to apply all the provisions of this Teaching" (D29:28).

Deuteronomy, Chapter 30

D30:1-10 – Moses tells the Israelites that if they stray from the

Lord's commandments and then repent and return, they will be even "more prosperous and more numerous than [their] fathers."
D30:11 – "Surely, this instruction which I enjoin upon you this day is not too baffling for you, nor is it beyond reach." Nevertheless, Moses goes over it all one more time, then concludes with: "I have put before you life and death, blessing and curse" (D30:19).

<u>Deuteronomy, Chapter 31</u>
Moses tells the Israelites that he's now 120, that Joshua must take over, that Joshua will be victorious and that "the Lord your God himself marches with you: he will not fail or forsake you." Moses then calls Joshua over and tells him to be "strong and resolute."
D31:9 notes that "Moses wrote down this Teaching and gave it to the priests."
D31:10ff – Moses instructs the Israelites that every seventh year, the year set for remission of debts, at the time of the Feast of Booths, the Teaching is to be read aloud in the presence of all Israel, including the children.
D31:14ff – God comes to Moses and tells him that it's almost time to die. He tells Moses to call Joshua and come to the Tent of Meeting, where the Lord then appears "in a pillar of cloud." God tells Moses that he, God, already knows that the people will break their covenant and that he'll get angry and abandon them. Even when they recognize that the reason for their problems is that God is not in their midst, God says, "Yet I will keep my countenance hidden that day, because of all the evil they have done in turning to other gods."

God then dictates to Moses a poem, which the Israelites are to read in their time of tribulation. Moses writes down the poem that very day and teaches it to the Israelites.
D31:23 – Moses again charges Joshua to be strong and resolute.

D31:25–29 – Moses gives the Levites "this book of Teaching" and tells them to put it beside the Ark and "let it remain there as a witness against you. Well I know how defiant and stiffnecked you are: even now, while I am still alive in your midst, you have been defiant toward the Lord; how much more, then, when I am dead!"

He calls the Levites together – all the elders of the tribes and all the officials – so that he can recite the poem to them.

Deuteronomy, Chapter 32

D32:1-43 is the poem. It's another litany of all the evils and horrors threats – some real, some metaphorical – that will befall the people if they stray from God's Commandments.

D32:45-47 – Moses tells everyone to take his warning to heart, for "this is not a trifling thing for you: it is your very life."

D33:48-52 – God calls Moses to the top of Mount Nebo to die, reminding him that he's not going to set foot in the promised land.

Deuteronomy, Chapter 33: Moses' farewell blessing to the Israelites. There is a special message to each tribe.

Deuteronomy, Chapter 34

Moses goes to the summit of Mount Pisgah to view the promised land before he dies. He is 120 years old when he dies, yet "his eyes were undimmed and his vigor unabated." The Israelites mourn him for 30 days.

D34:9 – Joshua takes over.

D34:10-11 – Torah ends with a brief encomium to Moses, e.g., "Never again did there arise in Israel a prophet like Moses – whom the Lord singled out, face-to-face."

Chapter Three
Good God!?
A Portrait of the Torah's Main Character

The main character in the Torah is, of course, God. Early on, he (and let's be very clear about it: in the Torah, God's persona is male) is quite prominent, creating the world, destroying it in a flood, and interacting with the various main characters in the narrative. He speaks with Abraham on several occasions, but he appears only occasionally throughout most of the latter part of Genesis as Isaac and Jacob live out their lives and Joseph is sold into slavery in Egypt. In Chapter 3 of Exodus, he reveals himself to Moses in a burning bush, and from there on, he occupies center stage.

If we use the Torah's record of God's thoughts, words, and actions, what do we find out about God? Is he worthy of worship? Of respect? Is he, as I have heard one purportedly humanist rabbi say from the pulpit, a representation of "sublime" human qualities, which the Torah writers invested in a divine figure so as to make it more likely that flawed humans would pay heed and conform?

Let's look at the text and see what kind of picture emerges.

(1) God and Moses[91] are annoyed, impatient, angry, and disappointed with the human race and (later) the Israelites.

- *Humanity is wicked.* G6:5-6 – "the Lord saw how great was man's wickedness on earth, and how every plan devised by his mind was nothing but evil all the

---

[91] In Deuteronomy, the voice is that of Moses, sometimes addressing the Israelites personally, sometimes giving God's message to them.

time. And the Lord regretted that he made man on earth, and his heart was saddened."

- ***Human aspirations must be punished.*** G11:5 – God sees the Tower of Babel and says, "If, as one people with one language for all, this is how they have begun to act, then nothing that they may propose to do will be out of their reach."

- ***God is so angry with the Israelites that he cannot bear to travel with them.*** E33:1-4 – After the incident with the golden calf, God promises the Israelites "a land flowing with milk and honey. But I will not go in your midst, since you are a stiffnecked people, lest I destroy you on the way." The Israelites get very depressed at this; they go into mourning, and no one puts on any "finery from Mount Horeb on."

- ***Humans are defiant, stiffnecked, and disobedient.*** In Deuteronomy, Chapter 9, an aggrieved Moses addresses the Israelites. He tells them that they are about to face the formidable Anakites and that "none other than the Lord your God is crossing at your head, a devouring fire; it is he who will wipe them out." Moses makes it very clear that God is giving them the land not because of their virtues but because of the wickedness of the other nations. God is dispossessing those nations to fulfill the oath that he made to Abraham, Isaac, and Jacob.

  Moses reminds them that they are a stiffnecked

people, that they provoked God to anger in the wilderness, and in fact "from the day that you have left the land of Egypt until you reached this place, you have continued defiant toward the Lord."

Moses recounts the entire incident of the golden calf. He says that God told him, "I see that this is a stiffnecked people. Let me alone and I will destroy them and blot out their name from under heaven, and I will make you a nation far more numerous than they."

Moses retells the story of how he smashed the tablets, fasted for 40 days and 40 nights, destroyed the golden calf by grinding it up and throwing its dust into a stream, and interceded for Aaron as well.

D9:22-23 – Moses recounts other occasions on which "you provoked the Lord...you flouted the command of the Lord your God; you did not put your trust in him and did not obey him." In fact (D9:24), "As long as I have known you, you have been defiant toward the Lord."

Later, (D31:25–29) Moses gives the Levites "this book of Teaching" – i.e., the Torah – and tells them to put it beside the Ark and "let it remain there as a witness against you. Well I know how defiant and stiffnecked you are: even now, while I am still alive in your midst, you have been defiant toward the Lord; how much more, then, when I am dead!"

- ***God has little faith in the Israelites' ability to keep his commandments.*** D31:14ff – God tells Moses that he, God, already knows that the people will break their covenant and that he'll get angry and abandon them. Even when they recognize that the reason for their problems is that God is not in their midst, God says, "Yet I will keep my countenance hidden that day, because of all the evil they have done in turning to other gods."[92]

(2) In the Exodus story, God plays both sides of the street, inflicting plagues on the Egyptians and – as the text notes several times – stiffening Pharaoh's heart so that the Egyptians' suffering can continue. All of this, as the text explicitly notes, is done for the sake of God's greater glory.

- E4:21-23 – God tells Moses that he is to "perform before Pharaoh all the marvels that I have put within your power." God also says that he'll stiffen Pharaoh's heart so that "he will not let the people go."

- E7:1-7 – God promises extraordinary punishments upon the Egyptians. Also: "I will harden Pharaoh's heart, that I may multiply my signs and marvels in the land of Egypt."

- E9:8-12 – God tells Moses and Aaron to take handfuls of soot and throw them skyward "in the sight of

[92] But see below, D30:1-10, where Moses says that if the people disobey and later repent, they'll be forgiven.

Pharaoh." The soot becomes "a fine dust all over the land of Egypt" and causes "an inflammation breaking out in boils on both man and beast..." God again stiffens Pharaoh's heart.

- E9:15-16 – God says that he could have killed all the Egyptians with pestilence but has spared them "in order to show you my power, and in order that my fame may resound throughout the world."

- E10:1-6 – God tells Moses that he, God, has hardened Pharaoh's heart so that he could display his power, and future generations will recount how he "made a mockery of the Egyptians."

- E10:20 - After the plague of locusts, God stiffens Pharaoh's heart.

- E10:27 – After the plague of darkness, God again stiffens Pharaoh's heart.

- E11:4-10 – Moses says that God has said that he will kill the first-born of all the Egyptians, including the cattle. But "the Lord had stiffened the heart of Pharaoh."

- E14:1-4 – Once the Israelites have escaped from Egypt, God tells Moses to tell them to turn back and encamp, so that the Egyptians will think they're lost. "Then I will stiffen Pharaoh's heart and he will pursue them, that I may gain glory through Pharaoh and all his host; and the Egyptians shall know that I am the Lord."

- **The parting of the Red Sea:** E14:15-18 – God tells Moses to lift up his rod and hold his arm over the sea "and split it, so that the Israelites may march into the sea on dry ground. And I will stiffen the hearts of the Egyptians so that they go in after them; and I will gain glory through Pharaoh and all his warriors, his chariots, and his horseman. Let the Egyptians know that I am Lord...."

(3) God (through Moses) indulges in displays of bragging and self-promotion.

- D4:32-40 – Moses' long and effusive tribute to God's works should be read in the original. Sample: "[E]ver since God created man on earth, from one end of heaven to the other: has anything as grand as this ever happened, or has its like ever been known? Has any people heard the voice of a God speaking out of fire, as you have, and survived?...".

- D:5-8 – Moses says that God's laws will be "proof of your wisdom and discernment to other peoples who on hearing of all these laws will say, 'Surely, that great nation is a wise and discerning people.' For what great nation is there that has a God so close at hand as the Lord our God whenever we call upon Him? Or what great nation has laws and rules as perfect as all this Teaching that I set before you this day?"

(4) God (through Moses) misstates the balance between what he does for the Israelites and what he does to them.

- D2:7 – "Indeed, the Lord your God is blessed you in all your undertakings. He has watched over your wandering through this great wilderness; the Lord your God has been with you these past 40 years: you have lacked nothing.[93]

(5) God is a Divine dealer: over and over, he offers land, health, fertility, and supremacy in exchange for loyalty.

- Genesis 17:4-8 – God makes Abraham "the father of a multitude of nations. I will make you exceedingly fertile and make nations of you; and kings shall come forth from you. I will maintain my covenant between me and you, and your offspring to come, as an everlasting covenant throughout the ages, to be God to you and to your offspring to come. I assign the land you sojourn in to you and your offspring to come, all the land of Canaan, as an everlasting holding. I will be their God."

- E23:25-33 – "You shall serve the Lord your God, and he will bless your bread and your water. And I will

[93] To me, this seems to be a pretty strange assessment of the 40 years, considering the plagues and other depredations.

remove sickness from your midst. No woman in your land shall miscarry or be barren. I will let you enjoy the full count of your days. I will send forth my terror before you, and I will throw into panic all the people among whom you come, and I will make all your enemies turn tail before you. I will send a plague ahead of you, and it shall drive out before you the Hivites, the Canaanites, and the Hittites...You shall make no covenant with them and their gods. They shall not remain in your land, lest they cause you to sin against me; for you will serve their gods – and it will prove a snare to you."

- E34:10-16 – God announces a covenant: "Before all your people I will work such wonders as have not been wrought on all the Earth or in any nation; and all the people who are with you shall see how awesome are the Lord's deeds which I will perform for you." God then announces that he'll undertake ethnic cleansing; he promises to drive out six different tribes and insists that the Israelites, even though they may be tempted to do so by the inhabitants of other lands, must not make any covenants with them: "No, you must tear down their altars, smash their pillars, and cut down their sacred posts."

- D6:20-25 – Moses: When your children ask the meaning of all the decrees, laws and rules, tell them it's because God freed us from Egypt and gave us the land he promised. Then he commanded us to observe all these laws "for our lasting good and for our survival."

- D7:6-8 – Moses says that the Lord chose Israel to be his treasured people, not because they're the most numerous ("indeed, you are the smallest of peoples") but "because the Lord favored you and kept the oath he made to your fathers" after freeing the Israelites from Egypt.

- D7:12-15 – "And if you do obey these rules and observe them carefully, the Lord your God will maintain faithfully the covenant that he made on oath with your fathers: he will favor you and bless you and multiply you; he will bless the issue of your womb and the produce of your soil, your new grain and wine and oil, the calving of your herd and the lambing of your flock in the land he swore to your fathers to assign to you. You shall be blessed above all other peoples: there shall be no sterile male or female among you or among your livestock. The Lord will ward off from you all sickness; he will not bring upon you any of the dreadful diseases of Egypt, about which you know, but will inflict them upon all your enemies."

- D9:7 – Moses makes it very clear that God is giving the Israelites the land not because of their virtues but because of the wickedness of the other nations. God is dispossessing those nations to fulfill the oath that he made to Abraham, Isaac, and Jacob.

(6) God (in Deuteronomy, through the voice of Moses) uses promises to encourage compliance.

- G15:17-21 – God makes the land-promise, the covenant with Abram. The rest of the chapter enumerates the tribes whose land God will give to Abram's offspring.

- G17:1-14 – God appears before Abram, now 99, and tells him that he will be "the father of a multitude of nations" and that his name is now Abraham. God promises land to Abraham's offspring, forever. Part of the bargain is circumcision at the age of eight days. This includes slaves. "Thus shall my covenant be marked in your flesh as an everlasting pact."

- G26:23-30 – God appears to Isaac and promises that "I will bless you and increase your offspring for the sake of my servant Abraham."

- G28:10-22 – God appears to Jacob in a dream and promises to him and his offspring the ground on which he is lying.

- G35:9-15 – God tells Jacob his name shall henceforth be "Israel," promises him the land he had assigned to Abraham and Isaac, and tells him that "Kings shall issue from your loins."

- G48:3ff – Jacob tells Joseph that God has appeared to him in a vision promising to make him "fertile and numerous" and giving his offspring the land of Canaan forever.

- E3:7-10 – After appearing to Moses in a burning bush, God tells Moses that he is aware of the Israelites' suffering and has come down to rescue them and bring them to a land of milk and honey; he enumerates the tribes whose land he's promising.

- E6:1-9 – God tells Moses to tell the Israelites that he, God, will free them "with outstretched arm and through extraordinary chastisements" and will bring them into the land which he swore to give to Abraham, Isaac, and Jacob.

- E15:22-26 – God promises that if the Israelites diligently keep all his laws, "then I will not bring upon you any of the diseases that I brought upon the Egyptians, for I am Lord am your healer."

- E19:1-6 – The Israelites encamp in the wilderness of Sinai. God tells Moses to tell the Israelites that "if you obey me faithfully and keep my covenant, you shall be my treasured possession among all the peoples...you shall become a kingdom of priests and a holy nation."

- E33:1-4 – God reiterates the promise he made to the patriarchs and enumerates the various tribes he's going to drive out; he promises the Israelites "a land flowing with milk and honey."

- D6: Moses enjoins the Israelites to "obey God's laws." The chapter provides the Israelites with various kinds of motivation to do so. Positive outcomes:

  D6:1 –"to the end that you may long endure."
  D6:3 –"that it may go well with you and that you may increase greatly [in] a land flowing with milk and honey."

- D6:16-19 – The Israelites are not to "try the Lord your God." They are to keep all his Commandments, decrees, and laws, so that "it may go well with you and that you may be able to possess the good land that the Lord your God promised on oath to your fathers, and that all your enemies may be driven out before you."

- D11:22-25 – Moses tells the Israelites that if they obey God's laws, God will "dispossess nations greater and more numerous than you," and their territory will extend "from the wilderness to the Lebanon" and from the Euphrates River to the Mediterranean Sea. D11:25 – "No man shall stand up to you: the Lord your God will put the dread and the fear of you over the whole land in which you set foot..."

- D26:16-19 is an exchange of affirmations: the Jews affirm that they will obey God, and God affirms that they are "his treasured people who shall observe all his commandments, and that he will set you, in fame and renown and glory, high above all the nations that he has made..."

- D28 begins with the blessings that the Israelites will enjoy if they obey God's Commandments.
  Some of the blessings are material: "Blessed shall be the issue of your womb, the produce of your soil" (D20:4); also, military victory (D28:7).

  Some are general: "Blessed shall you be in your comings and blessed shall you be in your goings" (D8:6).

  Some are metaphorical: "Blessed shall be your basket..." (28:5).

  D28:12 – Repeats the prediction that "you will be creditor to many nations, but debtor to none."

  D28:13 promises supremacy: "the Lord will make you the head, not the tail; you will always be at the top and never at the bottom..."

- D30:1-10 – Moses tells the Israelites that if they stray from the Lord's Commandments and then repent and return, they will be even "more prosperous and more numerous than [their] fathers."

(7) God (in Deuteronomy, through the voice of Moses) uses threats to encourage compliance.

- E34:4-8 – After the Golden Calf incident, Moses

carves a second set of tablets and goes up Mount Sinai. God passes before him and proclaims himself "compassionate and gracious, slow to anger, abounding in kindness and faithfulness, extending kindness to the thousandth generation, forgiving iniquity, transgression, and sin." Yet "he does not remit all punishment but visits the iniquity of parents upon children and children's children, upon the third and fourth generations." Moses bows low and begs God to go in their midst, "even though this is a stiffnecked people."

- D4:21-24 – Moses tells the Israelites that he's not going to cross the Jordan, so they had better not forget their covenant, "For the Lord your God is a consuming fire, an impassioned God."

- D8:19-20 – Moses tells the Israelites that "if you do forget the Lord your God and follow other gods to serve them or bow down to them, I warn you this day that you shall certainly perish."

- D28 is mostly a litany of curses and horrors that makes the previous one in Leviticus (see [8] below) seem mild. This one goes on for <u>52 verses</u>. It reverses all the blessings just given and then presents a long list of threats that are far more rich and detailed than the blessings, graphic to the point of ghastliness, e.g., 28:56-58 – "And she who is most tender and dainty among you, so tender and dainty that she would never venture to set foot on the ground, shall begrudge the husband of her bosom, and her son and her daughter, the afterbirth that issues from between her legs and the babies she bears; she shall eat them secretly, because of her want, in the desperate straits to which your enemy shall reduce you in your towns."

Or: "the Lord will inflict extraordinary plagues upon you and your offspring, strange and lasting plagues, malignant and chronic diseases" (D28:59-60).

Or: "The life you face shall be precarious; you shall be in terror, night and day, with no assurance of survival" (D28:66).

- D32:1-43 is another litany – this one in poetic form – of all the evils and horrors, some real, some metaphorical, that will befall the people if they stray from God's Commandments.

(8) God (in Deuteronomy, through the voice of Moses) threatens and promises at the same time.

- E20:5-6 – "I the Lord your God am an impassioned God, visiting the guilt of the parents upon the children, upon the third and upon the fourth generations of those who reject me, but showing kindness to the thousandth generation of those who love me and keep my commandments."

- E23:20-33 – God promises to send an angel to guard

the Israelites. He warns them against worshiping the gods of the peoples whose land he is going to give them. He promises blessings, fertility, and long life in exchange for loyalty. He tells the Israelites he's going to drive out the other peoples gradually so that the land will not become desolate. He warns them against making any covenants with the defeated peoples or their gods.

- E34:6 – God proclaims himself "compassionate and gracious, slow to anger, abounding in kindness and faithfulness extending kindness to the thousandth generation, forgiving iniquity, transgression, and sin. Yet he does not remit all punishment but visits the iniquity of parents upon children and children's children, upon the third and fourth generations."

- L26:3-13 – Benefits that the Israelites will receive if they obey God's commandments, e.g., "I will grant your rains in their season, so that the earth shall yield its produce and the trees of the field bear fruit...I will grant peace in the land, and you shall lie down untroubled by anyone."

  This is immediately followed by L26:14-45, a 30-verse litany of punishments that will rain down upon the Israelites if they disobey God, e.g., "You shall eat the flesh of your sons and the flesh of your daughters... I will spurn you. I will lay your cities in ruin and make your sanctuaries desolate, and I will not savor your pleasing odors. I will make the land desolate, so that your enemies who settle in it shall be appalled by it."

- D4:25-31 – Moses says that if the Israelites create any sculptured images, they're going to be wiped out and scattered "among the nations to which the Lord will drive you. There you will serve man-made gods of wood and stone, that cannot see or hear or smell." But if they seek God, he won't forget their covenant: "For the Lord your God is a compassionate God: he will not fail you nor will he let you perish."

- D5:9-10 – Moses tells the Israelites what God has told him: God has declared himself "an impassioned god" and promised to visit guilt upon third and fourth generations but to show kindness to "the thousandth generation of those who love me and keep my commandments."

- D6:10-15 – Moses reminds the Israelites that God is going to give them "great and flourishing cities that you did not build" as well as a lot of other things that they didn't earn, so they had better not forget God and had better revere only him, "for the Lord your God in your midst is an impassioned God – lest the anger of the Lord your God blaze forth against you and he wipe you off the face of the earth."

- D7:9-11– Moses says that God "keeps his covenant faithfully to the thousandth generation of those who love him and keep his commandments, but...

instantly requites with destruction those who reject him – never slow with those who reject him, but requiting them instantly."

- D11:13-17 – Moses tells the Israelites that if they obey God's Commandments, "You shall gather in your new grain and wine and oil. I[94] will also provide grass in the fields for your cattle and thus you shall eat your fill. Take care not to be lured away to serve other gods and bow to them. For the Lord's anger will flare up against you and you will soon perish."

- D11:26-28 – "See, this day I set before you blessing and curse: blessing, if you obey the commandments of the Lord your God that I enjoin upon you this day; and curse, if you do not obey the commandments of the Lord your God...".

(9) God claims the first-born children and animals and the first fruits of the harvest.

- E13:1-2 – God lays claim to every first-born, man and beast, among the Israelites.

---

[94] The switch to the first person is a bit confusing. JPS uses the first person pronoun but notes that the Samaritan version of the Torah has *he* (i.e., God).

- E22:28 – God gets the firstborn sons, as well as the first-born of all livestock.

- E23:19 – God gets "the choice first fruits of your soil."

- E34:19 – God lays claim to "every first issue of the womb." "None shall appear before me empty-handed."

- E34:26 – God lays claim to "the choice first fruits of your soil."

- N15:17ff – God commands Moses to tell the Israelites that when they enter the promised land, they are to set aside, as a gift to the Lord, "the first yield of your baking."

(10) God stages exhibitions of supernatural power to evoke awe.

- *God helps Moses work magic.* E4:1-9 – Moses is concerned that the Israelites won't believe him when he says he's going to lead them out of Egypt, so God tells him to cast his rod on the ground, whereupon it turns into a snake, then back to a rod. God tells Moses to put his hand into his bosom, and when he takes it out it's encrusted with snowy scales; he puts it back and takes it out again, and it's good as new. God says that if they don't believe these signs, Moses is to take some water from the Nile and pour it on the ground, and it will turn into blood.

- ***At Mount Sinai, God creates thunder, lightning, and smoke.*** E19:16-25 – On the third day after the Israelites arrive at Sinai, at dawn, "there was thunder, and lightning, and a dense cloud upon the mountain, and a very loud blast of the horn; and all the people who were in the camp trembled." The Israelites take their places at the foot of the mountain. "Now Mount Sinai was all in smoke, for the Lord come down upon it in fire; the smoke rose like the smoke of a kiln, and the whole mountain[95] trembled violently. The blare of the horn grew louder and louder. As Moses spoke, God entered him in thunder."

- ***More special effects at Mount Sinai.*** E20:15-18 – After God gives his commandments, "All the people witnessed the thunder and lightning, the blare of the horns and the mountain smoking; and when the people saw it, they fell back and stood at a distance. 'You speak to us,' they said to Moses, 'and we will obey; but let not God speak to us lest we die.' Moses answered the people,' Be not afraid, for God has come only in order to test you, and in order that the fear of him may be with you so that you do not go astray."

---

[95] JPS (p. 139 note *c*) observes that "some Hebrew manuscripts and the Greek read, 'all the people.'" Once again, the wide disparity between the two translations illustrates the difficulty of getting at the real meaning of the Torah text.

- *The* **manna** *as a symbol of God's power.* D8:3 – Moses tells the Israelites that God has "subjected you to the hardship of hunger and then gave you *manna* to eat, which neither you nor your fathers had ever known, in order to teach you that man does not live on bread alone, but that man may live on anything that Lord decrees."

(11) God uses his supernatural powers to help the Israelites fulfill the destiny he has mapped out for them.

- The Ten Plagues, E7ff.

- The parting of the Red Sea, E14.

- E15:22-26 – The Israelites come upon some water, but they can't drink it because it's too bitter. God tells Moses to throw a piece of wood into the water, which then becomes sweet.

- E16 – God provides nourishment in the form of *manna*.

- E17:1-7 – The Israelites encamp at Rephidim. There's no water, and they start quarreling and complaining to Moses. God tells Moses that when they arrive at the rock at Horeb, Moses is to strike the rock with his rod, and water will issue from it. He does, and the people drink.

- E17:8-16 – The Amalekites engage in battle with the

Israelites at Rephidim. Moses tells Joshua that he, Moses, will go to the top of a hill with "the rod of God" in his hand during the battle. When he holds up his hand, the Israelites prevail; when he lowers it, the Amalekites have the edge. Aaron and Hur hold Moses' hands up until the sun sets and Joshua overwhelms the Amalekites.

- N20:1-11 – The Israelites complain about their lack of water. God appears to Moses and tells him to assemble the community; God says that Moses will get water out of a rock.
  Moses hits the rock, out comes water.

(12) God makes liberal use of violence to punish disloyalty and disobedience.[96]

- God destroys almost all life on earth in a great flood (Genesis, Ch. 7).

- God annihilates Sodom and Gomorrah (Genesis, Ch. 19).

- ***A plague as punishment for the Golden Calf.*** E32:30-35 – After the Golden Calf incident, Moses[97] admits to

---

[96] In N20:12-13, God also punishes disloyalty by refusing to allow Moses and Aaron to enter the promised land "because you did not trust me enough to affirm my sanctity in the sight of the Israelite people."

[97] After instigating a Levite massacre of 3,000 Israelites as punishment for the disloyalty.

God that "this people is guilty of a great sin " and says that if God won't forgive them, he can "erase me from the record which you have written!" God tells him that that won't be necessary – but he does punish the Israelites with a plague.

- ***Incineration as punishment for improper ritual practice.*** L10:2 – God torches Aaron's sons because "they offered before the Lord alien fire, which he had not enjoined upon them."

- ***A fire as punishment for complaining.*** N11:1-3 – "The people took to complaining bitterly before the Lord. The Lord heard and was incensed: a fire of the Lord broke out against them, ravaging the outskirts of the camp. The people cried out to Moses. Moses prayed to the Lord, and the fire died down."

- ***A plague as punishment for complaining.***

N11:4-9 – "The riff-raff in their midst felt a gluttonous craving," missing the good food they had in Egypt; apparently they're getting dissatisfied with the manna, even though "it tasted like rich cream."

N11:10-15 – The people are weeping,"the Lord was very angry, and Moses was distressed." Moses begs God to help with deal with the people's anguished cries for meat.

N11:16-20 – God tells Moses to gather 70 of Israel's

elders and bring them to the Tent of Meeting, so that Moses doesn't have to bear his burden alone. God tells Moses that the Israelites will have meat for "a whole month, until it comes out of your nostrils and becomes loathsome to you."

N11:21-23 – Moses doubts that God can produce a whole month's worth of meat, but God answers, "Is there a limit to the Lord's power? You shall soon see whether what I have said happens to you or not!"

N11:31-34 – God creates a wind that sweeps quail from the sea and strews them "over the camp, about a day's journey on this side and one day's journey on that side...and some two cubits deep on the ground." The people start to eat the meat, but "the meat was still between their teeth nor yet chewed, when the anger of the Lord blazed forth against the people and the Lord struck the people with a very severe plague."

- ***Serpents as punishment for complaining.*** N21:4-9 – The Israelites complain about food and water, God sends serpents who bite them, and many people die. People come to Moses, beg him to intercede and get rid of the serpents. He does. Then God tells Moses to make a snake-like figure and "mount it on a standard. And if anyone who is bitten looks at it, he shall recover."

- ***Death as punishment for illicit sexual congress.***

N25:1-5 – Some Israelites profane themselves by whoring with the Moabite women, "who invited the people to the sacrifices for their god." God gets very angry and orders the death of the ringleaders: they are to be publicly impaled.

- ***A plague as punishment for illicit sexual congress.*** N25:6-9 – After the ringleaders are dead, one of the Israelites brings a Midianite woman into his tent, whereupon Phinehas, Aaron's grandson, stabs them both to death with his spear. This stops the current plague, which has claimed 24,000 lives.

- ***A death threat, denial of the Promised Land, and a plague as punishment for doubt.***

Numbers, Chapters 13-14 – God tells Moses to send scouts to check out "the land of Canaan, which I am giving to the Israelite people." After 40 days they come back with the report that the land is indeed flowing with milk and honey, but "the people who inhabit the country are powerful, and the cities are fortified and very large." The scouts (except Caleb) are intimidated, and they tell the other Israelites how formidable their best enemy is: "we looked like grasshoppers to ourselves, and so we must look to them."

N14:2 – "The whole community broke into loud cries, and the people wept that night. All the Israelites railed against Moses and Aaron." Joshua and Caleb and the other scouts tell the Israelites not to worry, that God will give them the land as promised. N14:10 – "As the whole community threatened to pelt them with stones, the presence of the Lord appeared in the Tent of Meeting to all the Israelites."

N14:11ff – God is really disappointed with the Israelites. After all the miracles he's performed, they still don't believe in him. He's also very angry. He's ready to "strike them with pestilence and disown them" – but Moses tells him that if he kills all the Israelites, people will think it was because he was unable to bring his people into the land he promised them. Moses begs God to pardon the Israelites, and God relents. *But...*

N14:21ff – God vows that no one who has "seen my presence and signs that I have performed in Egypt in the wilderness... shall see the land that I promised on oath to their fathers; none of those who spurn me shall see it," except Caleb.

N14:26ff – God decides that nobody over the age of 20 is going to make it to the promised land. The Israelites are sentenced to 40 years of wandering:

> "You shall bear your punishment for 40 years, corresponding to the number of days...that you scouted the land: a year for each day. Thus you shall know what it means to thwart me. I the Lord have spoken: Thus will I do to all that all that wicked band that has banded together against me: in this very wilderness they shall die to the last man."

N14:36 – Special punishment for the scouts who returned and spread "calumnies about the land": they die of plague, "by the will of the Lord."

- ***Death as punishment for disloyalty (N16).***

A group of 250 Israelites ("chieftains of the community"), motivated by Korah, Datham, Abiram, and On, rise up against Moses and Aaron for considering themselves holier than the rest of the people. Moses falls on his face.[98] Then he tells the group that the next morning, "the Lord will make known who is...holy, and will grant him access to himself." He tells the group to burn some incense in fire pans, and we'll see whom the Lord chooses. "You have gone too far, sons of Levi!" Plus, Moses says, you are already set apart by being Levites, with special access to God, as well as other honors: "Do

[98] JPS (p. 286, note *c*) suggests that another possible translation might be 'his face fell.'

you seek the priesthood too?"[99]

N16:12-15 – Moses sends for Dathan and Abiram, two of Israelites who instigated the uprising, but they refuse to come. Moses is very upset and tells the Lord to ignore their offering.

N16:16ff. – All 250 Israelites take their fire pans, put in fire in them, lay incense on top, and take their places at the entrance of the Tent of Meeting. God appears and tells Moses and Aaron to stand back "that I may annihilate them in an instant."

N16:22 – "But they [fall] on their faces" and beg for mercy: "when one man sins, would you be wrathful with the whole community?"

N16:25ff. – Moses instructs the Israelites to move away from the three instigators.[100] He tells them that "if these men die as all men do, if their lot be the common fate of all mankind, it was not the Lord who sent me. But if Lord brings about something unheard-of, so that the ground opens its mouth and swallows them up with all that belongs to them...you

---

[99] Regarding the difference between priests and Levites, Plaut (p. 1135) notes that "[t]wo classes of guards now protected the sacred precincts from all outsiders: priests, who were the chief officers and also have access to the inner court, and Levites who worked under their command."

[100] The text mentions only three; we don't find out what happened to On.

shall know that these men have spurned the Lord."

N16:32 – The Earth opens up and swallows them up with their households and possessions.

N16:35 – "And a fire went forth from the Lord and consumed the 250 men offering the incense."

N17:25 – God tells Moses that this incident is to be "[a]s a lesson to rebels, so that their mutterings against me may cease, lest they die."

N17:27 – The Israelites are really scared: "Lo, we perish! We are lost, all of us lost!"

- ***A plague as punishment for disloyalty.***

N17:2-12 – God orders Aaron's son to remove the fire pans ("for they have become sacred") and hammer them into sheets as plating for the altar – and to "serve as a warning to the people of Israel."

N17:6 – "The next day the whole Israelite community railed against Moses and Aaron," because they had brought death upon the people.

N17:8 – God appears and tells Moses and Aaron to remove themselves from the community, "that I may annihilate them in an instant." Moses tells Aaron to take the fire pans, add incense, and "make expiation for them. For wrath has gone forth from the Lord:

the plague has begun!"

N17:12 – Aaron makes expiation, and just in time too. 14,700 people die.

(13) God (in Deuteronomy, through Moses) is a war god who advocates violence and gives instructions for looting and pillage.

- N33:50-56 – God tells Moses that the Israelites are to completely destroy the Canaanites and take their land. If they don't completely annihilate the enemy, "those whom you allow to remain shall be stings in your eyes and thorns in your sides, and they shall harass you in the land in which you live; so that I will do to you what I planned to do to them."

- D7:1-5 – Instructions for the ethnic cleansing of "the land that you are about to enter and possess...seven nations much larger than you...you must doom them to destruction: grant them no terms and give them no quarter...you shall tear down their altars, smash their pillars, cut down their sacred posts, and consign their images to the fire."

- D7:16-26 – Moses tells the Israelites to destroy all the peoples that the Lord their God delivers to them, show the enemy no pity, don't worship their gods ("for that would be a snare to you"). Don't be afraid of them; just remember what God did to Pharaoh and the Egyptians. "Thus will the Lord your God do to all the peoples you now fear." He will also, among other punishments, send a plague against them "until those who are left in hiding perish before you."

D7:25-26 – "Consign the images of their gods to the fire," and don't "covet the silver and gold on them and keep it for yourselves, lest you be ensnared thereby...you must reject it as abominable and abhorrent."

- D12:2-3 – Moses tells the Israelites to destroy all of the other nations' worship sites, "tear down their altars, smash their pillars, put their sacred posts to the fire...".

(14) God administers harsh loyalty tests.

- ***The binding of Isaac.*** G22:1-14 – "God put Abraham to the test." He tells Abraham that he must offer his son Isaac as a burnt offering. Abraham obeys and begins preparations. He binds Isaac and is ready to kill his son, when an angel appears and tells him that he has passed the test. Abraham looks up, sees a ram, and offers it in place of his son.

  G22:15-19 – The angel calls to Abraham again and tells him that God has said that as a result of this show of loyalty, I will "make your descendants as numerous as the stars of heaven and the sands on the seashore; and your descendants shall seize the gates of their foes. All the nations of the earth shall bless themselves by your descendants, because you have obeyed my command."

- ***The forty years of wandering as a test.*** D8:2 reveals another reason for the forty years of wandering: "that he might test you by hardships to learn what was in your hearts: whether you would keep his commandments or not."

(15) God takes credit for humanity's accomplishments.

- D8:11-18 – Moses warns the Israelites not to forget that God is responsible for all the good things that have happened to them: "...beware lest your heart grow haughty...and you say to yourselves, 'My own power and the might of my own hand have won this wealth for me.' Remember that it is the Lord your God who gives you the power to get wealth..."

(16) God is not impervious to reason.

- G18:22-32 – Abraham bargains with God about the destruction of Sodom: "Will you sweep away the innocent along with the guilty?... Far be it from you to do such a thing, to bring death upon the innocent as well as the guilty." He gets God to concede that if there are as few as ten innocent people in the city, he won't destroy it.

- E32:9ff – After the Israelites create and worship the golden calf, God is ready to wipe them out. God tells

Moses, "'I see that this is a stiffnecked people..." and is ready to let his "anger...blaze forth and...destroy them." But Moses talks God out of destroying the Israelites. He argues that the Egyptians will say that God delivered the Israelites with evil intent only to kill them off. He reminds God about his promises to the patriarchs. "And the Lord renounced the punishment he had planned to bring upon his people."

(17) God (through Moses) pronounces a death sentence on anyone who practices any other form of religion.

- D13:2-6 – If there appears among you a prophet or a dream-diviner and he gives you a sign or portent, saying, 'Let us follow and worship another god'" don't do it, even "if a sign or portent that he named to you comes true." D13:6 – "As for that prophet or dream-diviner, he shall be put to death."

- D13:7-12 – Even if your wife or brother urges you to worship another god, don't do it. "Show him no pity or compassion, and do not shield him; but take his life" by stoning.

- D13:13-19 – The same harsh punishments for any Israelites who "[subvert] the inhabitants of their town: Doom it and all that is in it to destruction...Let nothing that has been doomed stick to your hand in order that the Lord may turn from his blazing anger and show you compassion, and in compassion increase you as he promised your fathers on oath...."

(18) God does have his better moments.

- ***A promise never to destroy the world again.*** G8:20ff – After God has destroyed the world in a flood, Noah builds an altar, and offers sacrifices to God, who smells the pleasing odor and says to himself: "Never again will I doom the earth because of man, since the devisings of man's mind are evil from his youth; nor will I ever destroy every living being as I have done."

- ***A blessing for Noah.*** G9:1-3 – God blesses Noah and his sons, tells them to be fertile and increase, and gives them dominion over all living things.

- ***Compassion for the poor.*** E22:25-6 – "If you take your neighbor's garment in pledge," you must return it before sunset. "In what else shall he sleep? Therefore, if he cries out to me, I will pay heed, for I am compassionate "

- ***Compassion for the downtrodden.*** D10:17-19 – Moses: "For the Lord your God is God supreme and Lord Supreme, the great, the mighty, and the awesome God, who shows no favor and takes no pride, but upholds the cause of the fatherless and the widow, and befriends the stranger, providing him with food and clothing."

- *Go and have a good time!* D14:22-26 – Moses tells the Israelites that they can consume their bounty in a place which God chooses (or, if it's too far, to convert it to cash, then spend the money "on anything you want – cattle, sheep, wine or other intoxicant, or anything you may desire").[101]

- *Generosity to the needy.* D15:7-10 – If there is a needy person among you, you must be generous, even if the year of remission of debts is approaching. D15:10 – "Give to him readily and have no regrets when you do so, for in return the Lord your God will bless you in all your efforts and other undertakings. D15:11 – For there will never cease to be needy ones in your land, which is why I command you, open your hand to the poor and needy kinsman in your land."

- *A call for fairness.* D16:19-20 – "You shall not judge unfairly: you shall show no partiality; you shall not take bribes, for bribes blind the eyes of the discerning and upset the plea of the just. Justice, justice shall you pursue, that you may thrive and occupy the land the Lord your God is giving you."

What About God?

Well, then, what about God? What kind of picture emerges

---

[101] This is the only time in the entire Torah that God actually tells the Israelites to go out and have a good time!

from God's words, thoughts, and behavior? What does the Torah text actually tell us?

This is a God who doesn't have much respect for human beings. He is an egomaniac who stages the entire Exodus drama to demonstrate his power. He brags about his own greatness and tells the Israelites that in their 40 years of wandering, "you have lacked nothing," despite all the plagues and other miseries he has inflicted upon them. He says that people are evil "from [their] youth," calls the Israelites stiffnecked (several times), and in fact doesn't have a single good thing to say about the human race.

Aside from creating the world, which he later destroys, God usually uses his divine powers to evoke awe or to inflict suffering and punishment on human beings.

He does a few positive things for the Israelites - e.g., the *manna* and the parting of the Red Sea - but only to get them to play out the destiny that he has laid out for them, i.e., to fulfill the land-for-loyalty promise he made to Abraham, Isaac, and Jacob. This deal is a constant theme in the Torah and a constant concern to God.

Compliance and obedience are extremely important to God. He encourages these qualities through promises and threats. He promises longevity, fertility, and supremacy. The threats are far more eloquent; both God and Moses describe in graphic detail how life will be hell for the disobedient.

God pronounces the death sentence on those who stray, and he often carries it out. He is completely intolerant of the practitioners of any other religion; their punishment is invariably death.

God can, on occasion, be reasoned with: Abraham manages to talk him out of annihilating the Sodomites, and Moses convinces him not to exterminate the Israelites.

There are about a half-dozen occasions on which he shows positive human qualities. (Of course, one could argue that the spirit of justice, fairness, and compassion which appears many times in the laws that Moses gives could also be counted as evidence of God's better nature – but I would reply that many of the laws are barbaric and irrelevant, so once again the data are mixed.)

In sum: the God of the Torah is certainly not worthy of worship - and rarely of respect. Except for a few moments of benevolence, he generally acts like the worst tyrants of modern times: vicious, vindictive, grandiose, and totalitarian. We have all known bosses like him.

The God that emerges from the Torah text is not surprising. In fairness to our ancestors, we must note that benevolent and enlightened rule was a rarity in their world, so they created an authority figure with the characteristics of the authorities they knew. And they were obviously at the lowest level of morality, since God's chief motivational tool is fear.

We would expect a primitive God to be the product of a primitive world. But what is surprising to me is the amount of human effort that has been expended in whitewashing and revising this God...all of the rabbi-hours spent in justifying and rehabilitating him.

Secular humanists are free of all this baggage. They accept the God of the Torah for what he is – and do not try to make him what he is not.

Chapter Four
How Relevant is the Torah to our Lives – Really?

A Classification of the Torah's Behavioral Directives

"Torah" means "teaching" – so what does the Torah really teach us? It has a powerful image as a repository of wisdom and profundity. But is it?

You can judge for yourself. In this chapter, I've assembled all of the Torah's behavioral directives - every case in which the text tells the people to do or not do something.

I was impressed by the breadth of these imprecations: there are directives on homosexuality, transvestitism, incest, urology, gynecology, warfare, military service, and much else, no doubt because the Torah's writers, priestly leaders of a rough and primitive society, were trying to teach people to act humanely and fairly in a variety of situations and thus to lay the foundations of morality (and hygiene).

The Torah does articulate some principles that have stood the test of time, but as we would expect, it falls far short of modern standards.

Its only punishments are death - employed far more liberally than in contemporary Western democracies[102] - and exile/ostracism. Women are almost always subject to the will of their fathers and husbands (although the remedies for rape and the rights awarded to divorced women are steps in the right direction). The Torah's many rules about agricultural practices, the treatment of slaves, and numerous other subjects are totally irrelevant to us.

---

[102] And in frequent contradiction of its command that "thou shalt not kill."

Some of its mandates are absolutely beyond our ken – see D25:11.

Finally, I should note that a very large number of the Torah's directives have to do with ritual and observance. God has highly specific requirements for his Ark, his temple, and his priests and their vestments, as well as a long shopping list of tributes and other goodies he requires. The Torah's elaborate attention to ritual is a mechanism for social bonding (see Chapter Five) as well as a way to create job security for the writers and other priests as well.

To assess the Torah's relevance to modern secular humanists, Jewish and otherwise, I've arranged all of its behavioral directives into four categories:

- those that deal purely with ritual;
- those that are of concern to the Israelites' primitive tribal society – but not to ours;
- those that touch upon broader moral concerns, even though the particular cases are irrelevant to us, e.g., penalties and compensation when someone is gored to death by an ox (E21:28);
- those that are of concern beyond a primitive society.

Here they all are. In some cases, I wasn't sure where to put a particular directive, and I've noted those cases in the footnotes. They are few in number. At the end, I'll have some comments on the relevance of the Torah to modern secular humanists.

Category I: Rules, regs and rituals; loyalty and obedience

G9:4 – "You must not... eat flesh with its lifeblood in it."

E12:1-20 – **Origin of the Passover ritual.** God tells Moses and Aaron to tell the Israelites to prepare a "passover offering"[103] – a lamb which they are to slaughter at twilight; its blood is to be put on the door posts of their houses.

They are to roast and eat the meat with unleavened bread and bitter herbs. They are to eat it hurriedly, with their sandals on and "your staff in your hand." This day is to be celebrated as a festival "throughout the ages." The Israelites are to remove all leaven from their houses and eat nothing leavened for seven days; anyone who disobeys will be cut off from the community.

E12:43-51 – The law of the Passover offering: No foreigner may eat it. A slave can eat it if he has been circumcised. So can strangers, if they and all their males are circumcised. E12:49 – "There shall be one law for the citizen and for the stranger who dwells among you."[104]

E13:1-2 – God lays claim to every first-born, man and beast, among the Israelites.

E13:3-8 – Moses repeats the instructions about eating unleavened

---

[103] Or "protective offering" (JPS, p. 122).

[104] This directive occurs several times in the Torah. From a modern perspective, it has been reinterpreted as a call for the protection of the rights of minorities. But <u>in context</u>, it is almost always clearly a mandate regarding the particular law or rule that is being articulated: the rule must be obeyed by both Israelites and strangers alike.

bread for seven days and celebrating a festival on the seventh day.

E13:9 – "And this shall serve you as a sign on your hand and as a reminder on your forehead."[105]

E13:11-15 – Instructions as to which first-born animals (but no children) are to be sacrificed.

E13:16 – "And so it shall be as a sign upon your hand and as a symbol on your forehead that with the mighty hand the Lord freed us from Egypt."[106]

E20:2-3 – "I the Lord am your God who brought you out of the land of Egypt, the house of bondage: you shall have no other gods besides me."

E20:4-6 – Do not make or bow down to sculptured images, for "I the Lord your God am an impassioned God, visiting the guilt of the parents upon the children, upon the third and fourth generation of those who reject me, but showing kindness to the thousandth generation of those who love me and keep my commandments."

E20:7 – Do not take God's name in vain.

---

[105] This is the commandment that has resulted in *tefillin* (aka phylacteries) – quite a leap, in my opinion. Reading the text yields no such instruction, and there is in fact no word or phrase – no antecedent, to use the appropriate grammatical terminology – to which "this" refers.

[106] See previous footnote. As with E13:9, there is no word or phrase to which "it" refers.

E20:8-11 – "Remember the Sabbath day and keep it holy."

E20:19-23 – God issues a prohibition against making any gods of silver or gold, and he gives Moses instructions for building an altar.

E22:19 – Condemnation of "whoever sacrifices to a god other than the Lord."

E22:27 – "You shall not revile God, nor put a curse upon the chieftain of your people."

E22:28 – God gets the Israelites' firstborn sons, as well as the firstborn of all livestock.

E22:30 – "You shall be holy people to Me."

E23:13 – Don't mention other gods.
E23:14 – Command to hold three festivals: the Feast of Unleavened Bread, the Feast of the Harvest, and the Feast of the Ingathering "at the end of the year, when you gather in the results of your work from the field."
E23:17 – "Three times a year all your males shall appear before the Lord."

E23:18 – Rules for making blood sacrifice.

E23:19 – God gets "the choice first fruits of your soil." Also, prohibition against boiling a kid
in its mother's milk.

E25: Instructions from God to Moses regarding the gifts that the

Israelites are to bring him; also, detailed instructions for the construction of the Ark, a table, and a lampstand of pure gold.

E26: Instructions for building the Tabernacle and the curtain behind which the Ark is to be carried.

E27: Instructions for building the altar and the enclosure of the Tabernacle. Also, instructions regarding the clear olive oil for kindling lamps which will burn "from evening to morning before the Lord. It shall be a due from the Israelites for all time throughout the ages."

E28: Instructions for creating the priestly vestments, as well as two stones engraved with "the names of the sons of Israel," a breastplate, and other priestly accouterments.

E29: Ritual instructions for ordaining priests, including the appropriate sacrifices.

E30:1-10 – Instructions for building an altar for burning incense; instructions for placement of the altar, burning incense, and purifying the altar.

E30:11-16 – God commands that each time a census is taken, a "ransom" shall be imposed on each Israelite "that no plague may come upon them through their being enrolled."

The remainder of the chapter contains instructions on combining spices to make a sacred anointing oil, plus instructions for using the oil in the proper manner.

E31:1-11 – God tells Moses whom he has assigned to make the various items previously enumerated.

E31:12-17 – Command to keep the Sabbath, under penalty of death, because God rested on the seventh day.

E34:17 – "You shall not make molten gods for yourselves."

E34:18 – Command to observe the Feast of Unleavened Bread.

E34:19 – God again lays claim to "every first issue of the womb." "None shall appear before me empty-handed."

E34:21 – Command to observe the Sabbath. (Also L19:3, D5:12-15, L23:3.)[107]

E34:22 – Command to observe the Feast of Weeks and Feast of Ingathering. E34:23 – "Three times a year all your males shall appear before the Sovereign Lord, the God of Israel."

E34:25 – A couple of rules on observing Passover.

E34:26 – Once again God lays claim to "the choice first fruits of your soil." Also repeats E23:19, the injunction against boiling a kid in its mother's milk.

E35-39: Begins with Moses reminding the Israelites to keep the Sabbath, on pain of death. Then Moses tells the Israelites to do everything that God said regarding the building of the Tabernacle and all its decorations. These instructions go on for all of chapters 35, 36, 37, 38, and 39.

---

[107] Again, no rationale is given except as a reminder to the Israelites that they were slaves in Egypt.

E40 – More instructions for setting up the Tabernacle and the Tent of Meeting.

L5:14-19 – Penalties for breaking the Lord's Commandments.

L6-9 – Instructions for the various kinds of sacrifices and burnt offerings.

L10:12-20 – More about the rules for sacrifice and where the sacrificial offering is to be eaten. (Moses is angry with Aaron's two remaining sons because they did not eat the sacrificial offering in the right place.)

L11 – **Dietary laws.** E.g., the Israelites may eat any land animal that has cleft hooves and chews cud. Of animals that live in water, they may eat only those that have fins and scales.

L16 – God dictates to Moses the ritual rules that Aaron must follow after the death of his two sons, whom God killed when "they drew too close to the presence of Lord"; God tells Moses what rituals Aaron must now practice.

L16:29-30 – Command to observe Day of Atonement. "The Israelites must practice self-denial and "do no manner of work."

L17 – More rules for ritual sacrifice. L17:13-14 – Prohibition against eating blood.

L18:2-5 – Prohibition against following any rules or laws but God's.

L18:21 – "Do not allow any of your offspring to be offered up to Molech."[108]

L19:14 – "You shall fear your God: I am the Lord."

L19:4 – No idols or molten gods.

L19:5-7 – Rules for sacrificial offerings.

L19:12 – Don't take God's name in vain.

L19:26 – Don't eat anything with its blood. Don't "practice divination or sooth saying."

L19:27 – "You shall not round off the side-growth on your head, or destroy the side-growth of your beard."

L19:28 – "You shall not make gashes in your flesh for the dead, or incise any marks on yourselves."

L19:37 – "You shall faithfully observe all my laws and all my rules:

---

[108] Plaut (p. 883) notes that there is some evidence that indicates that Molech could have been a heathen god (possibly, according to a later passage in the Book of Kings, the god of the Ammonites) to whom children were sacrificed.

I am the Lord."

L20:1-6 – Penalties for anyone who "gives any of his offspring to Molech"

L20:8 – Repeats 19:37.

L20:22-23 – Observe God's laws and not "the practices of the nation that I am driving out before you."

L20:26 – "You shall be holy to me, for I the Lord am holy, and I have set you apart from other peoples to be mine."

L20:27 – Death penalty for "a man or woman who has a ghost or familiar spirit." [109]

L21: This chapter consists mostly of instructions about how the priests, the sons of Aaron, are to conduct themselves.

L21:1-6 – Prohibition against defiling oneself on account of a dead kinsman.

L21:7 – Priests may not "marry a woman defiled by harlotry, nor shall they marry one divorced from her husband."

L21:9 – Death penalty for the daughter of a priest who defiles herself through harlotry.

---

[109] Meaning unclear, but may have something to do with divination (Hillman, p. 315).

L21:10-15 – Rules of conduct for priests (they may marry only a woman who is a virgin).

L21:16-22 – Nobody with a physical defect is allowed to "offer the food of his God."

L22 – More rules about who is allowed to partake "of any sacred donation that the Israelite people may consecrate to the Lord." Also, who may or may not "eat of the sacred donations." Animals offered for sacrifice must have no blemishes.

L23 – "the fixed times of the Lord, which you shall proclaim as sacred occasions."

L23:3 – Observe the Sabbath.

L23:5ff – Rules for observing Passover.

L23:9-21 – Rules for the harvest sacrifice.

L23:23-32 – Command to observe - and rules for observing- Rosh Hashana and the Day of Atonement.

L23:33ff – Command to observe the Feast of Booths. Rationale: to remind future generations that God made them live in booths during the Exodus.

L24:1-4 – Rules for setting up the kindling lamps outside the Tent of Meeting.

L24:5-9 – Rules for offering of bread and frankincense.

L24:10-16 – Story of a man who took God's name in vain. Penalty: death by stoning.

L26:1-2 – Don't make idols; keep God's Sabbath and venerate his sanctuary.

L27: Monetary values of the various items – animals, real estate, human beings – that are "vowed" or "consecrated" to God.

N6 – Ritual practices and obligations for nazarites.[110]

N7 – All the various chieftains of Israel assemble; this chapter describes the tributes/offerings presented by each one.

N8:1-4 – God's instructions about the hammered gold lampstand, before which are to be mounted seven lamps.

Rest of Chapter 8 – God's directives regarding the special status and duties of the Levites.

N9:1-14 – Instructions for offering the Passover sacrifice, with special rules for those who are "unclean by reason of a corpse" and for the "stranger who resides with you."

N10:1-10 – God tells Moses to make two silver trumpets, then tells him on what occasions they are to be sounded. "They shall be a reminder of you before your God: I, the Lord, am your God."

---

110 "Early exemplars of a holy life of separation and self discipline," Hillman, p. 362.

N15: Instructions for making a burnt offering or sacrifice and "producing an odor pleasing to the Lord."

N15:14 – Instructions for sacrificial ritual.

N15:22-29 – Instructions for expiation "if you unwittingly fail to observe any one of the commandments that the Lord has declared to Moses." But anybody who "acts defiantly reviles the Lord...[and] shall be cut off from among his people" (N15:30).

N15:37-41 – Commandments to make and wear a fringed garment: "look at it and recall the commandments of the Lord and observe them, so that you do not follow your heart and eyes in your lustful urge."

N18: Directions from the Lord to Aaron, regarding the privileges and duties of the Levites.

N18:20 – "You shall, however, have no territorial share among them or own any portion in their midst; I am your portion and your share among the Israelites."

N19:1-10 – Rules for sacrificing a cow.

N19:11-22 – More hygienic rules: how to purify yourself if you touch a human corpse.

N28:1-2 – God tells Moses to "command the Israelite people and say to them: Be punctilious in presenting to me at stated times the offerings of food due me, as offerings by fire of pleasing odors to me."

The rest of the chapter delineates various sacrifices, rituals, and obligations, including the Passover sacrifice and the command to eat unleavened bread for seven days. Also, a command to observe the Feast of Weeks.

N29: More rituals, required observances, and instructions for sacrifices. Command to refrain from work on the first day of the seventh month and the tenth day of the seventh month; on the latter occasion, Israelites are also to practice self-denial.

D4:8-18 – Moses tells them that since they've never seen God in any form, they are not to create "a sculptured image in any likeness whatever."

D4:19-20 – Don't worship the sun, the moon, or the stars; you are God's people.

D5:6-7 – I brought you out of the land of Egypt...have no other gods beside me.

D5:8ff – No sculptured images. God promises to visit guilt upon third and fourth generations but to show kindness to "the thousandth generation of those who love me and keep my commandments."

D5:11 –Don't swear falsely by the name of the Lord.

D11:18-21 – Remember God's words by binding them as a sign on your hand and forehead, teaching them to your children, and inscribing them on your door posts (repeats D4:8).

D12:1 – "These are the laws and rules that you must carefully observe in the land that the Lord...is giving you to possess, as long as you live on earth."

The rest of the chapter elaborates: Destroy all of the other nations' worship sites, "tear down their altars, smash their pillars, put their sacred posts to the fire...". Make sacrifices, tithes, contributions, and other "votive offerings" only in the places that God designates. Don't eat the blood of the animals you slaughter.

D12:29-31 – Do not inquire into or attempt to practice the religion of the nations whose land God has given you (D12:31 – "they even offer up their sons and daughters in fire to their gods").

D13:2-6 – If there appears among you a prophet or a dream-diviner and he gives you a sign or portent, saying, 'Let us follow and worship another God'" don't do it, even "if a sign or portent that he named to you comes true." D13:6 – "As for that prophet or dream-diviner, he shall be put to death."

D13:7-12 – Even if your wife or brother urges you to worship another God, don't do it. "Show him no pity or compassion, and do not shield him; but take his life" by stoning.

D13:13-19 – The same harsh punishments for any Israelites who "[subvert] the inhabitants of their town: "Doom it and all that is in it to destruction...Let nothing that has been doomed stick to your hand in order that the Lord may turn from his blazing anger and show you compassion, and in compassion increase you as he promised your fathers on oath...."

D14:1 – " You shall not gash yourselves or shave the front of your heads because of the dead."

D14:2 – Reference to Israelites as God's chosen people.

D14:3-21 – The familiar dietary laws, plus some not-so-familiar ones, e.g., "You shall not eat anything that has died a natural death."

D14:22-26 – Instructions to consume their bounty in a place which God chooses (or, if it's too far, to convert it to cash, then spend the money "on anything you want – cattle, sheep, wine or other intoxicant, or anything you may desire").

D14:27-29 – Instructions for contributions to the Levites, who don't have any hereditary land.

D15:1-3 – Instructions to practice, every seventh year, forgiveness of debts. "You may dun the foreigner; but you must remit whatever is due you from your kinsman."

D15:4-5 – If you only heed the Lord, there will be no needy among you.

D15:19-23 – Rules for consecrating to God the firstborn of the flock.

D16:1-8 – Instructions for observing Passover: no consumption of leaven; slaughtering the Passover sacrifice.

D16:9-17 – Instructions for observing the Feast of Weeks and the Feast of Booths. On these occasions, "all your males shall appear before the Lord your God in a place that he will choose. They shall not appear before the Lord empty-handed, but each with his own gift...".

D16:21 – Don't set up a sacred post near God's altar.

D17:1 – Don't sacrifice an ox or sheep that has any serious defect.

D17:2-7 – Procedures for rooting out worshipers of other gods and punishing them by stoning them to death. "Thus you will sweep out evil from your midst."

D17:18-20 – The king is to have a copy of "this Teaching" on a scroll, so that he can observe it faithfully, "to the end that he and his descendants may reign long in the midst of Israel."

D18:1-5 – Required donations to the tribe of Levi, the priestly class, e.g., special parts of each animal sacrificed.

D18:6-7 – Levites who go somewhere else ("to the place that the Lord has chosen") are still due their required portions and donations.

D18:9-14 – Do not imitate "the abhorrent practices" of the nations whose land God gives you, e.g., soothsaying, sorcery, spellcasting, "inquiries of the dead."

D18:15-22 – "The Lord your God will raise up for you a prophet from among your own people, like myself [i.e., Moses]." God will do this for them because they had asked it of him at Horeb. Furthermore, the Israelites are to put to death any false prophets, i.e., those whose prophecies do not come true, because they do not speak for God.

D21:1-9 – Ritual to be performed by the elders and magistrates to absolve the Israelites of blood-guilt if "someone slain is found lying in the open, the identity of the slayer not being known." Involves the sacrifice of a heifer that has never been worked.

D22:12 – Put tassels on the four corners of your garment.

D23:2 – "No one whose testes are crushed or whose member is cut off shall be admitted to the congregation of the Lord."

D23:3 – No *mamzer*[111] shall be admitted into the congregation of the Lord, not even to the tenth generation.

D23:4-7 – No Ammonite or Moabite shall be admitted into the congregation of the Lord, not even to the tenth generation, because "they did not meet you with food and water on your journey after you left Egypt, and because they hired Balaam to curse you." 23:6 – "But the Lord your God refused to heed Balaam... [and] turned the curse into a blessing for you...". 23:7 – "You shall never concern yourself with their welfare or benefit as long as you live."[112]

D23:8-9 – Don't abhor either Edomites (your kinsmen) or Egyptians, for you were a stranger in their land. Their children

---

[111] The meaning of the Hebrew word is uncertain, although in Jewish law, it refers to the offspring of adultery or incest between Jews (JPS, p. 377, note 3).

[112] Contradicts earlier directives about one law for Israelites and strangers alike.

may be admitted to the congregation in the third generation.[113]

D27:1-3 – Moses and the elders of Israel tell the people that as soon as they've crossed the Jordan, they're to set up large stones, coat them with plaster, and inscribe upon them all the words of "this Teaching."

D27:5-8 – Instructions to build an altar, make a sacrifice, rejoice, and inscribe every word "most distinctly."

D31:10ff – Moses instructs the Israelites that every seventh year, the year set for remission of debts, at the time of the Feast of Booths, the Teaching is to be read aloud in the presence of all Israel, including the children.

Category II: Laws/rules relevant only to ancient Israelites

E19:13 – "The wages of a labor shall not remain with you until morning."

E21:2-11 – Rules for buying and selling slaves, including rules for selling one's daughter into slavery.

E22:24 – Prohibition against charging interest.

E22:30 – Prohibition against eating carrion.

E23:10 – Principles of agricultural land management.

---

[113] I.e., of residence in Israel's territory; JPS, p. 378, note *c*.

L5:1-13 – Penalties for failing to testify, touching "any unclean thing," touching "human uncleanness," or " uttering an oath to bad or good purpose" (even though one doesn't recognize one's guilt at the time).

L12 – Rules concerning menstruation, purification and sacrificial offerings pertinent thereto.

L13 – Dermatological advice regarding leprosy and related matters. L13:45 – Lepers are required to call out "Unclean! Unclean!"

L14 – "The ritual for a leper at the time that he is to be cleansed."

L14:34 – What to do when "I inflict an eruptive plague upon a house in the land you possess," i.e., Canaan.

L15 – Urological advice. E.g., "When any man has a discharge issuing from his member, he is unclean." Instructions for avoiding contamination and contagion. L15:16-17 – What to do when a man has "an emission of semen."

L15:19ff – Gynecological advice and ritual. Who is clean and unclean, and under what conditions.

L17:14 – Prohibition against eating blood. Penalty: excommunication.

L19:19 – Observe God's laws. Don't "let your cattle mate with a different kind" or sow your field with two kinds of seed or "put on cloth from a mixture of two kinds of material."

L19:20-22 – What to do if "a man has carnal relations with a woman who is a slave and has been designated for another man, but has not been redeemed or given her freedom."

L19:23-25 – Wait five years before eating the fruit of any trees you plant.

L20:18 – No sex during menstruation.

L25:2-7 – Instructions for observing, every seventh year, "a Sabbath of the Lord ... a year of complete rest for the land."

L25:8-13 – Command to observe, every 50th year, a "year of jubilee." Instructions for buying and selling land in the year of jubilee.[114]

L25:23 – "[T]he land must not be sold beyond reclaim, for the land is mine; you are but strangers resident with me."

L25:25-28 – Legalities regarding recovery of the land sold to cover debts; special procedures in the jubilee year.

L25:29-34 – Same as preceding verses, but with regard to real estate.

L25:35-43 – Rules for fair treatment of one's kinsmen: "do not exact from him advance or accrued interest, but fear your God."

L25:44-47 – Rules pertaining to the sale and possession of "such male and female slaves as you may [have acquired]...from the

---

[114] The word comes from the Hebrew word for "ram."

nations round about you." L25:46 – "But as for your Israelite kinsmen, no one shall rule ruthlessly over the other."

L25:47-54 – Legalities regarding the right of redemption of one's kinsman who comes under the authority of "a resident alien among you."

N5:2-4 – "Remove from camp anyone with an eruption or discharge and anyone defiled by a corpse."

N5:11-31 – Ritual practices for situations in which neither a woman has gone astray or her husband has "a fit of jealousy," whether or not she has actually defiled herself.[115]

N19:11-22 – More hygienic rules: how to purify yourself if you touch a human corpse.

N27:1-11 – Several women, daughters of one man who died, beg Moses to allow them to inherit their father's property. Moses asks God, God agrees, and provides several other rules for the inheritance of property.

N30:4-6 – A woman's vows or obligations are subject to her father's approval while she is still in her father's household.

N30:7-9 – Same as the previous, except that the woman's vows are

---

[115] Hillman points out (p. 362) that "the test displaced spiteful or vindictive husbands as judges and juries of their wives [and]... honored a broader dictum that the weak were to be protected against the arbitrary exercise of power by the strong."

subject to her husband's approval. N30:14 – "Every vow and every sworn obligation of self-denial may be upheld by her husband or annulled by her husband."

N30:10 – The above does not apply to a divorced woman.
N31:19-24 – Instructions for cleansing and purifying after battle.

N31:25-54 – How the booty is divided among the Israelites.

N35:9-15 – God tells Moses that in the land of Canaan, "you shall provide yourselves with places to serve you as cities of refuge to which a manslayer who has killed a person unintentionally may flee... so that the manslayer may not die unless he has stood trial before the assembly."

N35:16-19 – If you hit anybody with an iron, stone, or wooden object and kill that person, you are a murderer and must be put to death.

N35:19 – "The blood avenger himself shall put the murderer to death."

N35:22-28 – If you kill someone unintentionally,"the assembly" will protect you and "restore [you] to the city of refuge to which [you] fled, and there...shall remain until the death of the high priest who was anointed with the sacred oil." You can't leave the city of refuge, because the blood-avenger can then kill you with impunity.

N35:30 – "If anyone kills a person, the man slayer may be executed only on the evidence of witnesses; the testimony of a single witness against the person shall not suffice for sentence of death."

N35:31 – "You may not accept a ransom for the life of a murderer who is guilty of a capital crime; he must be put to death."

N35:32 – "You may not accept ransom in lieu of flight to a city of refuge..."

N35:33 –"You shall not pollute the land in which you live;[116] for blood pollutes the land and the land can have no expiation for blood that is shed on it, except by the blood of him who shed it."

D15:12-18 – Rules for freeing one's slaves. D16-17 – If the slave wants to remain in your household, "you shall take an awl and put it through his ear into the door, and he shall become your slave in perpetuity."

D17:6 – "A person shall be put to death only on the testimony of two or more witnesses; he must not be put to death on the testimony of a single witness."

D19:11-22 – More hygienic rules: how to purify yourself if you touch a human corpse.

D17:8-13 – Procedures for handing over cases that are "too baffling for you to decide, be it a controversy over homicide, civil law, or assault" to "the levitical priests, or the magistrate in charge at the time." The priestly verdict is binding, under penalty of death: "Thus you will sweep out evil from Israel: all the people who hear will be afraid and will not act presumptuously again."

---

[116] On the face of it, this is simply a repetition of the command not to commit murder. It's not a statement about ecology.

D17:14-17 – If you want to have a king, it's OK with God, as long as God gets to choose the King. Make sure it's not a foreigner, and make sure that he doesn't "keep many horses or send people to Egypt to add to his horses, since the Lord has warned you, 'You must not go back that way again.'

And he shall not have many wives lest his heart go astray, nor shall he amass silver and gold to excess."[117]

D19:1-7 – Instructions to set aside three cities of refuge for a person who kills another unwittingly. Three cities are prescribed so that the accidental killer can reach one of them quickly.

D19:8-10 – You can add three more cities "when the Lord your God enlarges your territory, as he swore to your fathers."

D19:11-13 – Death penalty for premeditated murder, penalty to be administered by the "blood-avenger."

D19:14 – Don't move "your countryman's landmarks, set up by previous generations."

D19:15 – " [A] case can be valid only on the testimony of two witnesses or more."[118] Repeats D17:6.

D19:16-21 – Cases of suspected false testimony are to be submitted to magistrates, who will decide the truth of the matter. If a person

---

[117] This is another of those political passages; the purpose is to restrain the power of the king.

[118] Or perhaps three: meaning uncertain.

is deemed to have testified falsely, "you shall do to him as he schemed to do to his fellow... Nor must you show pity: life for life, eye for eye, tooth for tooth, hand for hand, foot for foot."

D20:1-9 – Psychological preparations for battle. Officials are to speak to the troops before the generals take over.

First of all, have no fear, because the Lord your God is with you, even if the enemy's forces are larger than yours. Those who are to be sent back home: anyone who has built a new house but not dedicated it, planted vineyards but never harvested, paid the bride-price for his wife but not married her. These individuals are to finish their tasks, lest they die in battle and someone else harvest their vineyard or marry their proposed bride. Also, if anyone is afraid and disheartened, he should go back home, "lest the courage of his comrades flag like his."

D20:10-18 – When you approach a town to attack it, offer terms of peace. If the inhabitants surrender, they "shall serve you at forced labor." If the town doesn't surrender, lay siege, kill all of its males, and take everything else as your booty.

The preceding applies to distant towns that "do not belong to nations hereabout." But if the towns are in territories that God has given you – the land of the Hittites, Amorites and Canaanites, among others – "you shall not let a soul remain alive...lest they lead you into doing all the abhorrent things that they have done for their gods...."

D20:19-20 – If you have to lay siege to a city, don't destroy its trees (except those that do not yield food).

D21:10-14 – Rules for what to do if one of your captives is a beautiful woman that you want to marry. You have to keep her for a month in your house – "after that you may come to her and possess her, and she shall be your wife." But if you don't want her anymore, you have to release her; you can't sell her or make a slave of her.

D21:15-17 – If you have two wives, "one loved and the other unloved," and the latter gives you your firstborn son, you still have to accept him and give him his birthright.

D22:5 – Prohibition against transvestitism. Whoever wears the clothes of the other gender "is abhorrent to the Lord your God."

D22:9 – Don't sow your vineyard with two different kinds of seeds.
D22:10 – Don't plow with an ox and an ass together.

D22:11 – Don't wear cloth that combines wool and linen.

D22:13-20 – Procedures for establishing the virginity of a woman whose husband becomes dissatisfied with her and claims she wasn't a virgin (involves producing the bloody cloth for the elders of the town). If the man is wrong, he is fined and flogged – and can never divorce the woman.

D2:20-21 – If he's right and she's not a virgin, she is to be stoned to death.

D22:23-28 – If a man has sex with a virgin who is engaged while she's in her town, both are to be stoned to death (because she didn't cry for help). However, if the rape occurs in the open country, "only the man who lay with her shall die." Also, a man who rapes a virgin who is not engaged has to pay the girl's father 50 silver shekels and marry her; he can never divorce her.

D23:1 – "No man shall marry his father's former wife..."

D23:10-15 – Instructions for conduct "when you go out as a troop against your enemies." Anyone who has had a nocturnal emission must leave the camp, bathe, and return only at sundown. D23:13-14 – Instructions for building a field latrine. D23:15-"Since the Lord your God moves about in your camp to protect you and deliver your enemies to you, let your camp be holy."

D23:18-19 – Prohibition against "cult prostitution"[119] by both men and women.

D23:20-21 – Prohibition against deducting interest from loans to your countryman. However, it's OK to deduct interest from loans to foreigners.

D24:1-4 – If a husband divorces his wife and she marries someone else, but the second husband divorces her or dies, the first husband can't marry her again.

D25:17-19 – Never forget how the Amalekites surprise-attacked you "when you were famished and weary."

Category IIa: Over-the-top

---

[119] Cult prostitutes performed sex as part of fertility or other cults, as opposed to common harlots.

Here are some examples of just how irrelevant to modern morality the Torah can be:

E21:15 – Death penalty for striking one's parents.

E21:17 – Death penalty for insulting one's parents.

D21:18-21 – A wayward and defiant son who does not obey his parents even after they discipline him shall be brought to a public place and stoned to death. "Thus you will sweep out evil from your midst: all Israel will hear and be afraid."

E22:17 – "You shall not tolerate a sorceress."

E22:18 – Death penalty for bestiality. Similarly, L20:15 – Death penalty for bestiality – both man and beast. L20:16 – Same penalty for both woman and beast.

L20:10 – Death penalty for adultery. Similarly, D22:22 – Death penalty for adultery – both participants.

L20:11 – "If a man lies with his father's wife...the two shall be put to death."

L20:12 – "If a man lies with his daughter-in-law, both of them shall be put to death."

L20:13 – Death penalty for homosexual relations between men.

D13 – Death penalty for urging the worship of other gods, even if the person is a close family member.

- D13:2-6 – "If there appears among you a prophet or a dream-diviner and he gives you a sign or portent, saying,' Let us follow and worship another God'" don't do it, even "if a sign or portent that he named to you comes true." D13:6 – "As for that prophet or dream-diviner, he shall be put to death."

- D13:7-12 – Even if your wife or brother urges you to worship another god, don't do it. "Show him no pity or compassion, and do not shield him; but take his life" by stoning.

D25:11 – "If two men get into a fight with each other, and the wife of one comes up to save her husband from his antagonist and puts out her hand and seizes him by the genitals, you shall cut off her hand; show no pity."[120]

<u>Category III: Moral strivings: Of limited relevance to modern times – but their heart was in the right place.</u>

G9:6 – "Whoever sheds the blood of man, By man shall his blood be shed;..."
E21:12-3 – Treatment of murder versus manslaughter.
E21:14 – Death penalty for first-degree murder.
E21:18 – Compensation for assault victims.
E21:20 – Penalties for beating or murdering slaves.
E21:22 – Penalties and compensation for injuring a pregnant

[120] My personal nominee for the strangest command in the Torah. Men's genitals were definitely taboo, it seems.

woman and causing miscarriage ("eye for eye, tooth for tooth").
E21:26 – Penalties for injuring one's slaves.
E21:28 – Penalties and compensation when one is gored to death by an ox.
E21:33 – Penalties and compensation when an animal falls into a pit.
E21:35 – Penalties and compensation when a man's ox gores his neighbor's ox.
E21:37 – Penalties and compensation for stealing livestock.
E22:4 – Penalties and compensation for letting one's livestock graze in another's land.
E22:5 – Compensation for damage from fire that one has started.
E22:6ff – How to handle situations when goods loaned to another for safekeeping are stolen: "both parties shall come before God: he whom God declares guilty shall pay double to the other."
E24:9ff – How to handle situations when one man gives livestock to another to guard, and the animal dies, is injured or stolen with no witnesses.
E22:13 – Compensation for loaned livestock that is injured.
E22:15 – Penalties and compensation for seducing a virgin.
E22:25-6 – "If you take your neighbor's garment in pledge," you must return it before sunset. "In what else shall he sleep?"[121]
E21:16 – Death penalty for kidnapping.
E22:30 – Prohibition against eating carrion.
E23:4 – You must return your enemy's ox or ass if either is found wandering off. Similarly, D22:4 – "If you see your fellow's ass or ox

[121] This is often interpreted as a command to serve the needy. But on the face of it, it's simply about returning borrowed goods, especially to a poor person. Anyway, it's one of God's better moments: "...if he cries out to me, I will pay heed, for I am compassionate."

fallen on the road, do not ignore it; you must help him raise it."
E23:5 – You must help your enemy if his ass is carrying too heavy a load.
E23:12 – Command to rest on the Sabbath.[122]
L5:20 – Penalties for situations in which "one person sins and commits a trespass against the Lord by dealing deceitfully with his fellow in a matter of a deposit or pledge, or through robbery, or by defrauding his fellow, or by finding something lost and lying about it"; what to do when one wants to "restore that which he got through robbery or fraud, or the deposit that was entrusted to him, or the lost thing that he found."
L18:6-20 – Rules for sexual conduct, e.g., "do not uncover the nakedness of your daughter-in-law: she is your son's wife; you shall not uncover her nakedness."
L19:13 – "[T]he wages of a laborer shall not remain with you until morning."
L20:14 – "If a man marries a woman and her mother, it is depravity; both he and they shall be put to the fire, that there be no depravity among you."
L20:17 – Penalty for incest between brother and sister is excommunication "in the sight of their kinsfolk."
L20:19-21 – Prohibitions against incest with various family members.
L20:25 – Separating the clean from the unclean.
L24:17 – "If anyone kills any human being, he shall be put to death."

---

[122] The reason given here is that one's livestock and "bondman and the stranger may be refreshed." There's nothing about God's resting on the seventh day.

L24:18 – "One who kills a beast to shall make restitution for it: life for life."
L24:19-20 – "If anyone maims his fellow, as he has done so shall it be done to him: fracture for fracture, eye for eye, tooth for tooth."
L24:21 – Repeats L24:17 and L24:18.
L25:17 – "Do not wrong one another, but fear your God: for I the Lord am your God."
N5:5-10 – Rules for making restitution for anyone who has committed a wrong and realized his guilt.
N19:11-22 – How to purify yourself if you touch a human corpse.
D16:18-20 – Instructions to appoint magistrates and officials to "govern the people with due justice."
D21:22-23 – If a man is guilty of a capital offense, executed, and impaled on a stake, the corpse cannot remain on the stake overnight; it must be buried the same day.
D22:6-7 – If you find a bird's nest with the mother sitting on the eggs or guarding the fledglings, "let the mother go, and take only the young, in order that you may fare well and have a long life."[123]
D22:8 – When you build a new house, make a parapet for the roof, "so that you do not bring blood guilt on your house if anyone should fall from it."
D23:16-17 – "You shall not turn over to his master a slave who seeks refuge with you from his master." He can live with you anywhere he chooses and must not be ill-treated.
D23:22-24 – When you make a promise to God, you must fulfill it.
D24:25-26 – When you enter another man's vineyard or grain field, you can eat as much as you want to but don't collect any and take it with you.

---

[123] I wasn't sure about how to classify this one, but it does seem to have some moral force behind it, so I gave it the benefit of the doubt.

D24:5 – A man who gets married gets a one-year exemption from military service "to give happiness to the woman he has married."
D24:7 – Death penalty for kidnapping "a fellow Israelite, enslaving or selling him."
D24:8-9 – If someone gets a skin disease, "be most careful to do exactly as the levitical priests instruct you."
D24:10-13 – "When you make loans of any sort to your countryman, you must not enter his house to seize his pledge" (presumably a garment; see what follows). 24:12 – "If he is a needy man, you shall not go to sleep in his pledge; [24:13 –] you must return the pledge to him at sundown, that he may sleep in his cloth and bless you..."
D24:15 – "You must pay [a needy and destitute laborer] his wages on the same day, before the sun sets, for he is needy and urgently depends on it; else he will cry to the Lord against you and you will incur guilt."
D24:16 – "Parents shall not be put to death for children, nor children be put to death for parents: a person shall be put to death only for his own crime."
D24:19 – When you reap your harvest and overlook a sheaf, don't go back to get it. It goes to "the stranger, the fatherless, and the widow."
D24:20-21 – The same thing applies to the fruit of your olive trees and the grapes of your vineyard.
D26:12 – Give one-tenth of your yield to the Levites, the stranger, the fatherless, and the widow.

Category IV: Relevance beyond the tribal society of the ancient Israelites – more or less universal significance.

E19:13 – Prohibition against fraud or robbery.

E20:12 – Honor your father and mother.
E20:13 – "You shall not murder...commit adultery...steal...[or] bear false witness against your neighbor."
E20:14 – "You shall not covet..."
E22:20 – "You shall not wrong a stranger or oppress him, for you were strangers in the land of Egypt." Also E23:9 – "You shall not oppress a stranger, for you know the feelings of the stranger, having yourselves been strangers in the land of Egypt." L19:33-34 – Love the stranger as one of your citizens because you were strangers in the land of Egypt. N9:14 – "There shall be one law for you, whether stranger or citizen of the country." D10:19 – "You too must befriend the stranger, for you were strangers in the land of Egypt."
E22:21 – "You shall not ill-treat any widow or orphan." ("My anger will blaze forth and I will put you to the sword.")
E23:1 – "You must not carry false rumors; you shall not join hands with the guilty to act as a malicious witness."
E23:2 – "You shall neither side with the mighty to do wrong – you shall not give perverse testimony in a dispute so as to pervert it in favor of the mighty – [E23:3] – nor shall you show deference to a poor man in his dispute."
E23:6 – "You shall not subvert the rights of your needy in their disputes."[124]
E23:7 – "Keep far from a false charge; do not bring death on those who are innocent and in the right..."
E23:8 – "Do not take bribes..."
L5:1-13 – Penalties for failing to testify, touching "any unclean thing," touching "human uncleanness," or "uttering an oath to bad

---

[124] Sort of repeats E23:2.

or good purpose" (even though one doesn't recognize one's guilt at the time).

L18:6-20 – Rules for sexual conduct, e.g., "do not uncover the nakedness of your daughter-in-law: she is your son's wife; you shall not uncover her nakedness."

L18:23 – Prohibition against bestiality.[125]

L19:2 – "You shall be holy, for I the Lord your God, am holy."[126]

L19:3 – Honor your father and mother.

L19:9-10 – Leave the gleanings of your harvest and the fallen fruit of your vineyard for the poor and the stranger. Also L23:22 – Leave grain for the poor. L19:11 – Don't steal or "deal deceitfully or falsely with one another."

L19:14 – "You shall not insult the deaf, or place a stumbling block before the blind."

L19:15 – Show fairness to rich and poor alike; "judge your kinsman fairly."

L19:16 – "Do not deal basely[127] with your countryman. Do not profit by the blood of your fellow: I am the Lord."

L19:17 – "You shall not hate your kinsfolk in your heart. Reprove your kinsman but incur no guilt because of him."

L19:18 – "You shall not take vengeance or bear a grudge against your countryman. Love your fellow as yourself: I am the Lord."

L19:29 – "Do not degrade your daughter and make her into a harlot, lest the land fall into harlotry and the land be filled with depravity."

---

[125] I really wasn't sure where to put this one.

[126] I wasn't sure about this one either, but it sounded like a general commandment to be good, so I gave it the benefit of the doubt.

[127] The meaning of this phrase and of *profit by* are uncertain.

L19:35 – "You shall not falsify measures of length, weight, or capacity."
L19:36 – More on honest weights and standards.
L24:22 – "You shall have one standard for stranger and citizen alike."
L25:17 – "Do not wrong one another..."
L35:39-43 – Do not make a slave of your kinsman if he must live with you because he is in dire circumstances.
N30:3 – Command to keep one's vows, oaths, and self-imposed obligations.
D5:16 – Honor your father and mother.
D5:17 – No murder, adultery, theft, or bearing of false witness.
D5:18 – Do not covet.
D15:7-10 – If there is a needy person among you, you must be generous to him, even if the year of remission is approaching.
D15:10: "Give to him readily and have no regrets when you do so for in return the Lord your God will bless you in all your efforts and other undertakings. D15:11 – For there will never cease to be needy ones in your land, which is why I command you, open your hand to the poor and needy kinsman in your land."
D16:20 – "You shall not judge unfairly: you shall show no partiality; you shall not take bribes, for bribes blind the eyes of the discerning and upset the plea of the just."
D16:20: "Justice, justice shall you pursue, that you may thrive and occupy the land that the Lord your God is giving you."
D22:1-3 – You must try to return missing items, such as an ox or sheep gone astray, or a garment or "anything that your fellow loses and you find: you must not remain indifferent."
D24:6 – "A hand mill or an upper millstone shall not be taken in pawn, for that would be taking someone's life in pawn."
D24:14-15 – Don't abuse a needy and destitute laborer, whether an

Israelite or not.
D24:17 – "You shall not subvert the rights of the stranger or the fatherless; you shall not take a widow's garment in pawn."
D25:13-16 – Injunction to practice honest weights and measures.

Morality 101

One way to assess the Torah's relevance is to ask how many of its numerous directives consist of advice that modern secular humanists can follow.

To answer this question, we must set aside all the material on ritual (which, by my rough estimate, accounts for at least a third of all of the Torah's directives), as well as all the material that is of interest mainly or exclusively to ancient Israelite society. These directives are irrelevant to us without a certain amount of (and, in some cases, a lot of) rabbinical spin.

The category that is of interest to humanists is IV – transcendent moral principles. On the basis of my reading of the Torah text, devoid of interpretation or spin, the number of Torah principles that humanists can conscientiously apply – and by the most generous count[128] – is about 30. Here they are:

(1) Don't commit fraud (E19:13; L5:20 – penalties for fraud).

(2) Don't carry false rumors or act as a malicious witness (E23;1); "keep far from a false charge" (E23:7); don't deal deceitfully (L19:11); don't bear false witness (E20:13; D5:11).

---

[128]There are some passages in which the Torah simply prescribes the penalties for particular offenses, e.g., Leviticus, Chapter 5. I counted these as directives not to do the behavior in question.

(3) Don't commit robbery (L19:13).

(4) Honor your parents (E20:12, L19:3, D5:17).

(5) Don't commit murder (E20:13, D5:17).

(6) Don't commit adultery (E20:13, D5:17).

(7) Don't covet (E20:14).

(8) Don't steal (E20:13, L19:11, D5:17).

(9) Don't wrong or oppress the stranger (E22:20, L19:33-4, N9:14, D10:19, D 24:17).

(10) Don't ill-treat widows or orphans (D24:17).

(11) Don't deal basely(?)[129] with your countrymen (L19:16); don't hate them even though you reprove them (L19:17).

(12) Be impartial in disputes (E23:2-3,6; L19:15); pursue justice (D16:19-20).

(13) Don't take bribes (E23:8, D16:19).

(14) Don't fail to testify (L5:1).

(15) Don't touch anything unclean (L5:2).

(16) Don't have sex with family members (L18:6-20).

(17) Refrain from bestiality (L18:23).

(18) Be holy (L19:2).

(19) Be generous to the needy; leave gleanings for them (L19:9-10, L 23:22, D15:7-10); don't abuse a needy or destitute laborer (D24:14-15).

(20) Be kind to the disabled (L19:14).

(21) Don't make your daughter a harlot (L19:29).

(22) Don't be vengeful (L19:18).

(23) Don't bear a grudge (L19:18).

(24) Love your fellow as yourself (L19:18, L25:17).

(25) Practice fair and honest weights and measures (L19:35,

---

[129] The meaning of the Hebrew is uncertain.

36; D25:13-16).

(26) Don't make a slave of your kinsman who is in dire straits (L35:39-43).

(27) Keep your vows (N30:3).

(28) Try to return lost items (D22:1-3).

(29) Don't take the means of someone's livelihood in pawn (D24:6); don't take a widow's garment in pawn (D24:17).

None of the items in Category IV is news to me. As a humanist, I've been trying to practice fairness, compassion, and all the rest for many years, long before I knew what the Torah said about all these matters.

Beyond that, the Torah has a considerable amount of material that deals with moral issues in a primitive context. Many of its directives, although the specifics are of little interest outside the context of ancient Israelite society, embody such basic humanistic principles as fairness and compassion. However, much of the material - e.g., the many directives on the treatment of slaves and the severe strictures on the rights of women - does not square with our modern sensibilities.

As I pointed out in the previous chapter, secular humanists are quite comfortable with this kind of thing. Once again, the Torah is what it is. It's a valuable window on the world of our ancestors. We've made a lot of moral progress since Biblical times (though we still have a long way to go).

Secular humanists don't have to spin the Torah so that it and/or God can appear to offer deep moral messages for our time. We can credit our ancestors with developing a rudimentary moral code (which may have borrowed from other, earlier ones) and leave it at that.

We should give the Torah writers credit for a good first draft of morality and hygiene. They used both carrot and stick, especially fear of God's wrath, to get the Israelites to behave well (and also to carry out a long list of religious rituals).

The fact is that they weren't the only ones - or even the first ones - to get it right. Other societies of the time were more advanced in their moral thinking.

My conclusion can only be that the Torah's moral content is vastly overrated. Since Biblical times, there's been a wealth of Jewish culture, learning, and experience, as well as much profound thought, Jewish and otherwise, on morality and conduct. When it comes to thinking about right and wrong, secular humanists have vast and magnificent resources to draw upon.

Let's give the ancient texts their due – and move on.

APPENDIX
The Jews in the Ancient World

Eugene Finerman

[The Torah was written well before humanism emerged in the ancient world. Humanistic thought does make an appearance in ancient Jewish life, albeit after the Torah was written: as Rabbi Sherwin Wine has pointed out, one of the roots of modern Jewish humanism is the call for social justice by the prophets of the eighth century BCE.

However, it has been my contention throughout this book that a secular humanist should have no problem whatsoever with the

> *Torah's anti-humanistic bias, its primitiveness, or the fact that its moral imprecations are largely irrelevant to modern times. The humanist alternative to spinning the Torah is to simply accept it for what it is - and to understand why it is what it is. In the following essay, historian/satirist Eugene Finerman explains that the Jews were one of the more backward peoples of the ancient world and that in fact they resisted the sophisticated and humanistic cultures which they encountered. — AMP]*

No Pharaoh would recognize the culture or language of modern Egypt. Pericles would not identify with or understand the modern Greek. Julius Caesar might recognize the aquiline nose and the hedonism in the modern Italian, but he'd be mystified by the "new" religion and the loss of the imperial identity. Hillel, however, would find in the modern Jew a consistency and continuity in religion and culture. When you consider the great empires and civilizations of Antiquity, it is a remarkable irony that the sole surviving culture would be a humble, parochial, tribal society.

Does that seem a harsh description of the ancient Jews? It is the Torah's definition. The Jews were depicted as the descendants of nomads and slaves. In fact, there is a historical basis for such humility. As early as 1850 B.C.E., Mesopotamian archives speak of marauding nomads known as the Hapiru. Four centuries later, when the Egyptian Empire extended into Canaan, the Pharaohs campaigned against the incursions of tribes known either as the Apiru or Habiru. Pharaoh Amhotep II (c. 1427 to 1400 B.C.E.) lists among his military triumphs the capture and enslavement of 3,600 Apiru. It was not a decisive victory, however. The cities of Canaan repeatedly appealed for Egyptian help against the Habiru invaders. Although the Canaanite and Egyptian records never allude to any theological idiosyncrasies among these nomads, there is little doubt as to who the Habiru were and would become.

The Bible revels in the hardscrabble Bedouin culture of the Jews. Their enemies - the Canaanites and the Philistines - lived in cities, an indication of their corrupt natures. Of course, the Jews would eventually conquer these cities, but observance of the Torah would maintain the Jews' fundamentalist purity. When Solomon built the Temple, he had to hire the necessary artisans and artists from Phoenicia, a culture that did not discourage "graven images" or other aesthetics.

According to the Bible, under David and Solomon, the Jewish kingdom grew rich and powerful. It is historically possible. By the 11th century B.C.E., Egypt was in decline. To the north, the Hittite Empire had disintegrated. There was no great power to restrict the growth of the Jewish state. Yet, despite the Biblical depiction of a mighty Jewish nation, there is no contemporary evidence that David and Solomon even existed. Egypt, even in decline, was still a literate and sophisticated society, with a bureaucracy of scribes who would have recorded on time-withstanding papyrus the diplomatic and commercial contacts of the kingdom. Phoenicia certainly was a literate society; indeed, its alphabet was to become the basis of our own. At the very least, you'd think an invoice for Solomon's Temple might have survived. No such evidence has yet been uncovered.

As the Bible asserts, there were indeed two Jewish kingdoms - Judea and Israel - by the 9th century BCE. Ironically, their existence was verified by their conquerors. The Assyrians kept gleeful records of the tribute that they extorted from the Jewish states. In the British Museum, you can see the Assyrian murals depicting the fall of Lachish, the second largest city of Judea. Assyria destroyed the kingdom of Israel. Babylonia conquered both Judea and Assyria. In turn, Persia conquered Babylonia and restored a degree of autonomy to its Jewish province.

In *The Histories,* written in the 5th century B.C., Herodotus included a catalog of the provinces and cultures of the Persian Empire. The Greek historian describes Phoenicia and mentions the old Philistine city of Gaza, but makes no reference to Jerusalem. Indeed, he says nothing about the Jews, at least by name. He briefly refers to the area as "Coelosyria" – Greater Syria — and his only acknowledge of the inhabitants' culture is their practice of circumcision. Their unique theology and its stringent code of observances go unnoticed.

Alexander's conquests finally acquainted Hellenism with Judaism. The Greeks were not impressed but optimistically assumed that the Jews would gratefully adapt to the superior culture. Who would want to adhere to a backward tribal code when offered the genius of Hellenism? The Jews' refusal to assimilate—even to the point of revolt under the Maccabees—left the rebuffed Greeks with the lasting disdain for the stiff-necked, irredeemably barbaric Jews.

In time, the Romans acquired Judea and the Greeks' prejudices. The poor soil of Judea and rich opportunities abroad had encouraged Jews to enter commerce and move throughout the empire. Nearly one third of Alexandria's population was Jewish. Rome's first synagogue was established in approximately 45 B.C.E. Perhaps as many as 40,000 Jews lived in Rome at the beginning of the first century. The Jews were very much a part of the cosmopolitan life of Rome, but not an esteemed part. Their beliefs and observances made them the subject of a satire by Juvenal. The 1st century wit ridiculed

> *Some, whose lot it was to have Sabbath-fearing fathers,*
> *Worship nothing but the clouds and the numen of the heavens,*

And think it as great a crime to eat pork, from which their parents
Abstained, as human flesh. They get themselves circumcised,
And look down on Roman law, preferring instead to learn
And honor and fear the Jewish commandments, whatever
Was handed down by Moses in that arcane tome of his…"[130]

Such is the verdict in a dead language of a ruined Empire. "That arcane tome" is the Jews' covenant with history. As both an epic and a liturgy, the Torah has given the Jews their identity and meaning. With that covenant, we Jews have withstood time and tyranny.

---

[130] *Satires*, XIV, 96-103; translated P. Green.

Chapter Five
Understanding What the Torah Really Says: Why It Matters

A Secular Humanistic View of the Torah

A secular humanistic view of the Torah acknowledges the truth of the following propositions:

- The Torah document that we use today is the product of four separate documents involving a number of authors and at least one editor who compiled the four documents into one. The Torah was probably complete by the fourth century BCE, but it underwent further editing by Masoretic scholars to better preserve the meaning. The document used in most synagogues dates from the 10th century CE, some 1,300 years after the Torah was first compiled in its present form.

- The original Torah stories were written for political as well as philosophical and genealogical reasons; we see politics, for example, in the passages that set forth the limitations on kings or postulate *ad hoc* histories that justify, centuries later, the second-tier status of Esau's and Aaron's descendants (because Esau had given up his birthright and Aaron had been compliant in the disastrous Golden Calf incident).

- The God of the Torah exhibits humanistic virtues on several occasions, but for the most part he is a vicious and violent tyrant.

- There is no external corroboration – historic, archaeological, or linguistic – for any of the events in the Torah. There is no independent historical account of the Jews in Egypt, as slaves or in any other role. The Exodus did not occur as the Torah describes it, although some of the place names are real, and the story does have some parallels with actual events: Nomadic Semites called *Hapiru* or *Apiru* (ultimately from Mesopotamia) encroached on the Egyptian Empire, attacking Egypt's allies and tributary states in Canaan, but not the kingdom itself. The Pharaoh Thutmosis III (reigned *c.* 1458-1427 B.C.E.) fought them and captured and enslaved many of them. Amhotep, another Pharaoh from the same century, counts among his military triumphs the capture and enslavement of 3,600 Apiru. Thus, as Finkelstein and Silberman suggest, the Torah's account of enslavement and emancipation may have been written from the geo-political perspective of a later age.[131]

- There is no external evidence that any of the Torah's individual characters existed (though later portions of the Bible do have some actual historical content); similarly, there is no reason to believe that any of its

---

[131] Chapter 2, *The Bible Unearthed: Archaeology's New Vision of Ancient Israel and the Origin of the Sacred Texts,* by Israel Finkelstein and Neil Silberman (New York: Simon & Schuster), 2001.

numbers are accurate – for example, there's simply no way that 600,000 people could have crossed the desert and left no trace.

- Of the Torah's many commandments, those that are relevant to us number only a few dozen; these consist of nothing more than basic moral behaviors that today are part of growing up civilized.

I can't see anything about the above points that a secular humanist would have serious problems with (and of course, no secular humanist believes that God or Moses wrote the Torah).

At this point a skeptical secular humanistic Jew (or any secular humanistic skeptic, for that matter) might ask: So? What does it matter whether people ignore the original Torah and sit around reading other people's stories (and making up their own stories) about it, if that gives them comfort and makes them feel that they belong, makes them feel Jewish and religious?

The answer is that the comfort, the belonging, the Jewishness, and the religiosity come at a high price that humanists are unwilling to pay: the Torah believer is required to abandon certain key humanistic virtues and habits of mind, whereas the humanistic view of the Torah enables and encourages us to practice these same qualities.

The Torah and Humanistic Virtues

Here is what secular humanists practice (and uncritical Torah lovers do not practice) when they think and talk about the central symbol of their Jewish heritage:

Realism and honesty. Humanists are realistic and honest about what the Torah says. We cheerfully acknowledge that it is indeterminate, inconsistent, and primitive. At the same time, we regard it as an important source of information about how our ancestors lived and how they viewed their world. Most important of all, intellectual honesty requires us to refrain from twisting and spinning the Torah until it says what we want it to say.

For many Torah enthusiasts, the most ancient Jewish stories are the most appealing, the most comforting. To produce this feeling of comfort, they make the Torah say what it does not say. They invest the characters in these ancient stories (including God) with qualities that they do not have. They trade honesty for comfort.

Courage. In a world where 95% of the people believe in God and even those who don't believe that God wrote the Torah still consider the document profound and relevant, it takes real courage to believe and speak the truth about the Torah. And it takes courage to cut through all the spin and to face and accept the truth of what the Torah really says.

On a broader scale, it takes quite a bit of courage to acknowledge that there is no divine hand or plan guiding our destiny and that God will not take care of us if only we pray loud and hard and long enough, even if we obey his multitudinous commandments and laws to the letter.

Dignity. As we would expect, the Torah gives short shrift to human dignity. Personal liberty and women's rights are unknown. Obedience to God is unquestionably the dominant theme, and with very few exceptions, the Torah provides no express reason for doing anything other than that God says to do so. But secular humanists prefer to spend their time with writers and thinkers who value human dignity and show us how to promote it.

Respect for science and reason. It is through science and reason that we search for truth. Through science and reason we learn, to the extent possible, who really wrote the Torah and what it really says.

Respect for our Jewish heritage. We Jews are the inheritors of a 4,000-year-old culture and tradition. The Torah is the first written record of that tradition. To respect it is to try to understand what it actually says and to credit it with the moral insights that it contains. To disrespect the Torah is to "interpret" it, to change it, to make of it what it is not.

What Humanists Should Do with the Torah

Put it in the library with the other books.

For those who want to know more about the Torah, there are many books that explicate such issues as its origins, its authorship, its relation to history and myth, and so on.[132]

If this kind of inquiry makes one feel more Jewish, fine. But it is only one way to express one's Judaism. I myself would prefer to become better acquainted with modern secular Jewish philosophers, novelists, and poets.

Religion and Comfort

I freely acknowledge that one of the purposes of religion is to give comfort in a chaotic and often hostile world. It fascinates me that religions offer a veritable supermarket of comfort options. You can wrap leather straps around your arms because somebody said that that's what the Torah says to do (as we saw, it doesn't), or you can ingest a tasteless wafer and pretend it's the body of a god. Sometimes the rituals take the form of physical mutilation or

---

[132] Two excellent places to start are Finkelstein and Silberman's book and *Who Wrote the Bible?* by Richard Elliot Friedman (New York: HarperCollins Publishers), 1997.

tortuous rites of passage.

It's all about comfort: the comfort of having questions answered, of knowing what to do each moment of the day, of being able to face your own death, of belonging.

Those are important needs, and people will go to great lengths to fulfill them. Freud and Marx thought that religious behavior was simply madness, but it turns out that there's more to it than that. People will engage in the most bizarre and irrational rituals because these constitute behavior that is, in the words of Richard Sosis writing in *American Scientist*,[133] "too costly to fake." Sosis says,

> "There is no incentive for nonbelievers to join or remain in the religious group, because the cost of maintaining membership – such as praying three times a day, eating only kosher food, donating a certain part of your income to charity and so on – are simply too high."

I think "too costly to fake" is a wonderful way to put it. To paraphrase an important Jewish philosopher, Groucho Marx, I would never lay *tefillin* in order to be a member of a group of folks who would lay *tefillin*!

But everyone should take religious comfort where he or she can find it. And where one finds it is a very personal decision. Perhaps it's baked into our individual DNA. In any event, the result is what I call Perlman's Law of Subjective Real Estate.

The phenomenon has been noted many times before. Author Anaïs Nin observed that "we see things not as they are, but as we are."

Here's my version: we occupy the same physical/external

---

[133] Volume 92, March-April 2004.

real estate but vastly different psychological/internal real estate. A theist is just as certain that God exists as I am that he does not. On this subject, our subjective worlds are non–contiguous (and this difference is, as far as I'm concerned, way beyond discussion), even as we inhabit the same physical world.

And our individual minds perceive no difference between the two. For me the proposition that God does not exist is as true as the proposition that I am staring at a computer screen as I write this.

But being a secular humanist is what gives me comfort.

For one thing, it's a great liberation: I don't have to worry about what God wants, what God thinks, what God's plan is for me or for the world, what God is saying (or not saying) to me, what God really meant in this or that Bible passage, or whether God will answer my prayers. I'm free of all that baggage.

Being around other secular humanists gives me comfort. Ours is, as Rabbi Wine liked to say, a "horizontal" religion – salvation comes from within and from each other, not from above this world or from beyond this life.

Since I'm not praying to God (or thinking about him at all), I have more energy to invest in cultivating humanistic virtues, so as to improve myself, my relations with others, and my environment. I work to make the most of each day, because I believe that when you're dead, you're dead, and we have only this one chance.

If I'm not mistaken, the bottom line in many religions, stripped of all the God-baggage and ritual, is that one should cultivate humanistic virtues to improve one's life on this earth, as well as the lives of others. It would seem that much of the rest is done for the sake of comfort and belonging.

When it comes to the Torah, secular humanists see an opportunity to practice their religion. I'm willing to sacrifice a little comfort: the comfort of belonging to the majority, the comfort of believing that the Torah's ancient stories are profound and relevant and that our ancestors were far wiser than we and that they have answers to all of our questions.

I'm willing to give up that comfort for the sake of courage, science and reason, honesty, dignity, intellectual integrity, truth, and respect for my Jewish heritage.

I don't think it's too high a price to pay.

Afterword I: Honest Language Usage – the semantics of "God"

What does it mean to "believe in God"?

As a linguist and a Jew, I've thought about this question for many years and listened to how people answer it.

One answer is that God is an omniscient, omnipotent supernatural being who communicates with people and intervenes in earthly events - not unlike the God of the Torah (whose violent and vindictive streak has been whitewashed by centuries of clerical "commentary" and who now appears in movies as George Burns or Morgan Freeman).

Another answer is "Cosmological God" – he/she/it created the universe and set the laws of nature in motion, but that's it. This version of God doesn't talk to people or intervene in human history. Nevertheless, there are educated, sophisticated people who believe in Cosmological God yet still attend prayer services.

Cosmo, as I like to call him, has a couple of big selling points: prayer and ritual aren't necessary, and he's compatible with evolution.

Beyond this, the semantics start to get a bit slippery. This is the "many definitions of God" school of thinking. God is love, God is nature, God is the ground of being, God is *gaia*, God is my feeling of awe at the universe, God is the infinite potentiality that underlies all matter and energy...the list is endless.

People who define God this way are ignoring the fact that we already have names for all of these items: *love, nature, the ground of being,* and so forth.

By declaring that one of these things is God, one is saying, "this is very, very important to me." Such a declaration also sounds (at least to me) like an implicit message to the people who believe in "Bible God" (i.e., the vast majority), a message that says something like "Hey, don't exclude me - I believe in God too."

"God is love" and all other such expressions are a way of subtly avoiding "Bible God" and "Cosmological God" – but not rejecting God.[134]

Afterword II: Honest Language Usage – the semantics of "spiritual"

Nowadays everybody wants to be spiritual, including humanists. I think the logic is the same as in the previous paragraphs: no one wants to be cut off from the majority.

"Spiritual" used to mean "of the spirit," i.e., the non-material. A monk or a nun would have been considered an example of a spiritual life. Excessive materialism and consumerism are still considered "non-spiritual."

Today, "spirituality" also denotes the practice of – and often

---

[134] The same applies to self-proclaimed humanists who spin the Torah and character of God.

a concern with the mythology and cosmology) of – religions other than the Western Big Three.

The word can also be used loosely to refer to any psychological or philosophical concern, as with Zen.

We also have non-theistic spirituality, of several kinds.

A spiritual state can be a state of love, ecstasy, connectedness, and total absorption in the moment, as with meditation or artistic performance (as well as religious ritual).

Spirituality has also been identified with humanistic virtues. Norman Shealy, M.D., Ph.D., in his book *Sacred Healing,* identifies such "attributes of spirituality" as forgiveness, tolerance, serenity, compassion, charity, confidence, courage, reason, and wisdom.

In my opinion, the meaning of "spiritual" has been broadened for social and cultural reasons: to allow many more people to say they're "spiritual." As with "God," the new definitions convey to me an air of desperate me-tooism, because being identified as "spiritual" has such positive social value.

Some Jews act as if spirituality consists of spinning the Torah and talking about God's supposed virtues, without actually praying to or believing in God. I disagree. This is a superficial spirituality that violates humanistic values.

www.ingramcontent.com/pod-product-compliance
Ingram Content Group UK Ltd.
Pitfield, Milton Keynes, MK11 3LW, UK
UKHW041431210726
13854UKWH00010B/1853